S0-BFB-328

Fishing in the Comfort Zone

Choosing Fishing Techniques, Tackle,
and Locations to Make Your Fishing
Experience More Enjoyable with an
Emphasis on Light Tackle Fishing from
Kayaks and Other Small Boats

John Veil

Preface

Over the past three decades spent as a fisherman, I caught thousands of fish representing many species. Each year I strive to catch new species and to earn some personal bests on species I have caught before. While some other anglers are far more skilled than me in their fishing techniques and others consistently catch larger fish than me, I still catch plenty of fish. I learn from reading books and Internet board posts by others, by fishing with guides, and most of all by spending a lot of time on the water fishing and observing. I am not yet an expert fisherman, but I continue to learn and improve.

I have done a great deal of technical writing in my professional career working on water and energy subjects. I often write fishing reports and offer suggestions to others on Internet fishing boards. But I have not previously attempted to collect my thoughts on fishing in a single document. This book represents my first effort at a fishing book.

Nobody has the time or talent to be a good fisherman in every style of fishing. Clearly there are basic fishing skills that carry over from one form of fishing to another, but a person who is an expert in trolling offshore for marlin is not necessarily an expert in fly fishing for trout or casting lures for largemouth bass or muskies. Each style of fishing and each fishing location and environment require specialized skills, equipment, and lots of practice in order to excel. Likewise, few anglers are interested enough or have the financial resources to pursue all forms of fishing with equal gusto. Each of us must make decisions on how to fish, where to fish, and what type of gear to use. That is the main theme of this book. To most enjoy fishing, try to learn those aspects of fishing that you like and those that you do not like. These will help you find the sweet spot or "comfort zone".

In introducing this book, I want to acknowledge several people. First, I am grateful to my wife Carol for giving me a green light to fish nearly any time I want to go. I hear many other anglers gripe about having to get spousal permission to go fishing. With only a few exceptions, I can plan my fishing schedules without checking in first.

Second, I am fortunate to have found a group of friends and fishing buddies who share my passion for fishing – we have similar fishing interests and have enough time to fish together frequently on week days. During the past year seven of us formed a casual group we call the Old Guys Who Like to Fish (OGWLF). The core members of this group include Mark Bange, Terry Hill, Harry Steiner, John Rentch, Scott Taylor, and Bruce Kellman. Several other guys join us occasionally, but those named above are the most active OGWLF members. We share fishing reports and often plan joint outings. Over the years I often fished alone. It is a pleasure to have other like-minded guys with whom I can share experiences and fishing trips.

I single out OGWLF member and friend Mark Bange for his encouragement and support in writing this book. Mark reviewed and edited a draft of the book. His comments were extremely helpful. He also provided supplemental material to bolster descriptions of baitcasting and fly fishing equipment and allowed me to use some of his photos in the book.

I am grateful for the opportunity to get exposed to new ways of fishing and new fishing destinations. I particularly thank Doug Dixon (Alaska, north woods of Maine) and Virgil Poe (ice fishing and pickerel tutoring) for getting me to fishing locations I never would have gone on my own.

Most of the photos included in the book were taken by me. Several photos were provided by friends with their permission. A few photos, particularly the ones that show me with fish, were taken by someone else who used my camera. I cannot recall who took those photos, so no credits are given.

Warning: Fishing can be addictive. Use the information and tips from this book wisely. Don't blame the author for your excessive expenditures on fishing trips and gear or for unhappy family members who no longer see you often enough.

CONTENTS

Part One:
The Fishing
Comfort Zone

Chapter 1 – What is "Fishing in the Comfort Zone"?

In July 1993 I was in the Florida Keys with my family. A friend and I booked a half-day flats charter with a local guide who worked at the hotel's marina. In those days I fished some at home in Maryland but was not particularly skilled at casting. The guide watched me casting one of his spinning reels for the first few minutes of the trip then told me he would not let me fish anymore unless I learned how to cast his way. He proceeded to show me his way of casting and insisted that I do it that way. He was not encouraging or coaching in his approach -- he was bossy and cranky.

I complied with the instructions and undoubtedly did cast better after that. But what I remember from that day is that he imposed his will and fishing technique on me, even though I was a paying customer. I have little recollection of what we caught, if anything, but I will never forget the crusty old guide treating me in a heavy-handed way.

That story is a great starting point for this book. With the exception of those who earn their living from fishing (e.g., guides, charter captains, commercial watermen, and professional tournament anglers) nearly all of us fish because we enjoy fishing, not because we have to fish or depend on fish for as a main source of income or food. For most of us, fishing is something we do to get away from the responsibilities and stress of everyday lives. If we are forced to fish in ways with which we are not comfortable using tackle that is not suited to our skills, we are less likely to enjoy the trip. Likewise, if we lose concentration or interest in fishing after a few hours but are forced to stay out on the boat for many more hours (think of kids or spouses), we are unlikely to have a positive memory of the day. Throughout this book I describe fishing techniques and gear that I have tried and explain whether I found them to fall within my comfort zone or not.

The "Best" Fishing Technique or Gear

I want to emphasize clearly at the start of the book that <u>I do not believe there is any universal "best" fishing technique or "best" type of tackle</u>. One type of rod, reel, or lure may be *your* best or favorite choice, but it may not be the best choice for others. Tackle manufacturers want you to believe that their products are superior to those offered by their competitors. They have compelling advertisements and endorsements by famous anglers to show how great their products are. Well-known fishing authors and seminar speakers offer their thoughts and opinions on methods, tackle, gear tweaking, and locations to fish. By all means, learn from these experts. But don't be afraid to fish in your own way, even if it differs from the advice given by the experts. In line with this sentiment, I hope that readers will consider the thoughts and advice offered in this book, but then choose which of my ideas to accept and which ones to ignore. As much as I would like to believe that I have all the right answers, it simply is not true.

There are many ways to catch fish. Some anglers like to use all or many of those techniques at different times. Others have narrowed down their scope of fishing methods to find those that best meet their skill set and interest. There are many Chesapeake Bay fishermen who are outstanding at trolling with heavy tackle and at livelining spot for stripers[1]. They have great success catching many fish and large fish. Many other anglers greatly enjoy fly fishing for its challenges and the opportunity to fish with the flies that they tied themselves. These are all respected and productive techniques. However, I personally do not particularly enjoy fishing using those techniques and therefore I spend no time fishing that way. There is nothing wrong with those fishing techniques, but they fall outside my fishing comfort zone.

---

[1] I use the terms "striped bass" and "stripers" interchangeably throughout the book.

Likewise, some anglers love to own and fish with many types of rods, reels, lines, and lures. That is great if you enjoy trying to choose just the right combination for the conditions where you are or if you like lure collecting or having lots of "fishing stuff" in your garage or man cave. Alternatively, if you exclude some types of equipment and focus your attention on specific tackle types, you can simplify your personal collection of tackle.

Some anglers love fishing at dozens of different locations and spend hours on the road getting there. This clearly brings variety – it is appealing to some anglers to experience many different environments and try to catch different species. However, it also spreads your available fishing time around and may inhibit your ability to gain seasonal knowledge of individual bodies of water. There is nothing wrong with either approach – it is personal preference.

That is the key message of this book – to best enjoy your personal fishing experience, you should find ways to fish, types of tackle, and locations for fishing that meet your own set of interests and criteria, rather than trying to do it all. These criteria include:

- *Your budget for fishing.* Fishing can be expensive, particularly if you fish from a large boat, outfit it with electronics and lots of tackle, tow it, and keep it fueled up. Bait, ice, fishing licenses, ramp fees, and insurance will drive the cost up. On the other hand, simple shoreline fishing can have minimal cost. My brother fishes from the banks of streams and lakes near his home in Pennsylvania using inexpensive tackle and gets a great deal of enjoyment fishing in that simple way.

- *The amount of time you are willing to devote to fishing considering your family, job, and other interests.* Sometimes the most desirable fishing is several hours away from where you live. In order to drive to the launch point, ride to the fishing grounds, spend your time on the water, then return home, you can put in some very long days. Another aspect of time commitment is how long you can remain comfortable physically and sharp mentally. Some anglers are good to go for long trips. Others (like me) prefer half-day trips that better suit my attention span and allow me to keep active before old-guy aches and pains take over.

- *The interests and availability of your fishing buddies.* It is best to find fishing buddies who have similar interests and schedules to your own. Those interests do not have to overlap completely, but you should share some core interests. If you love to troll with heavy tackle and your buddy mainly wants to fly fish, you will have some conflicts on where to go and how to spend your fishing time. Also, fishing on weekdays offers less boat traffic and competition for the fish that are out there. If your fishing buddies all have Monday-to-Friday jobs while you are retired, there will be fewer opportunities to fish together.

- *How you get to the fish.* Some anglers fish mainly in their own boat or on a buddy's boat. Others prefer to hire a guide or charter captain for most of their trips. If you have your own boat, how large does it need to be to meet your needs? Do you need a special vehicle powerful enough to tow the boat? Many anglers (me included) are fishing often from small, easily transported vessels like kayaks or canoes. Still others prefer fishing without a boat at all – they fish from a shoreline, pier, beach, or may wade to fish.

When you have fished enough to know which techniques and fishing locations you enjoy and those that you do not like or cannot afford, you can begin to define your fishing comfort zone. In the following chapters I describe different techniques, tackle, and locations that I have tried over the years and explain why I placed them within my own fishing comfort zone or elected to exclude them from future consideration. For those techniques and tackle that I do enjoy and use often, I provide much more discussion and description to explain not only what I do, but why I do it.

I want to state clearly that no way of fishing, as long as it complies with relevant regulations, is bad or inferior. All too often different sectors of the fishing world tend to look down upon or dismiss those who choose to fish in ways other than how they do it. There have been and will continue to be conflicts between:

- Trollers vs. light tackle fisherman
- Fishing using artificial lures vs. bait vs. flies
- Those who practice catch-and-release vs. those who keep every legal fish they catch
- Freshwater vs. saltwater fishing
- Those with expensive boats vs. those with older, smaller boats or kayaks.

Many youngsters and those who are fishing purely for relaxation take great delight in catching small panfish by hanging a piece of earthworm beneath a bobber. Most persons who read this book have moved on to fishing techniques that require more personal skill and effort to find and catch fish. But there is no reason to dismiss the pure fishing fun that simple techniques can provide.

In finding your fishing comfort zone, you will necessarily discard or rule out some fishing techniques, some types of tackle, and some potential fishing locations. Those items are not inherently bad – they may be within someone else's comfort zone. It is also quite possible that your comfort zone will expand or contract over the years as your interests change.

Information Resources for Learning about Fishing and Refining Your Comfort Zone

I mentioned fishing authors earlier in this paragraph. I do not have a huge fishing library. My personal fishing library for the Chesapeake Bay region contains two books by Shawn Kimbro ("Chesapeake Light Tackle" and "The Right Stuff"), one by Lenny Rudow ("Rudow's Guide to Fishing the Chesapeake"), a kayak fishing book by Alan Battista ("Light Tackle Kayak Trolling the Chesapeake Bay"), and an older book on striped bass by Keith Walters ("Chesapeake Stripers"). For fly fishermen, Joe Bruce has written a series of books on fly fishing. All of these men are excellent fishermen and good writers. I hope my book can approach the level of usefulness that their works have provided to many anglers in our region.

As we move steadily into the electronic media era, many anglers are providing useful information through their own websites and blogs, through fishing chat boards, and through videos. Of these media types, I frequently post on regional fishing chat boards, but do not have a fishing blog or website, nor do I produce fishing videos.

There are various regional or local fishing organizations or clubs that meet periodically through the year. Frequently those clubs invite local fishermen or guides to speak at their meetings. During 2015, I spoke at meetings of the Coastal Conservation Association (CCA) – Patuxent River Chapter, Maryland Saltwater Sportfishermen's Association (MSSA) – Broadneck Chapter, and the Free State Flyfishers Club. In addition to these groups, different businesses or organizations sponsor fishing seminar series. As an example of this, I spoke at a fishing seminar series at the Bass Pro Shops in Hanover, MD in the spring of 2014. These events occur on an ongoing basis and can be a great way to learn from more experienced anglers and to talk to them in person.

Chapter 2 – My Fishing Comfort Zone

Throughout my fishing years I have made more than a thousand fishing trips in varied locations and have fished using many different techniques and different types of tackle. Through those experiences, I have been able to get a pretty good sense of how I like to fish, where I want to fish, and when I want to fish. In this chapter I explain why I like certain fishing activities and do not choose to fish using other approaches.

<u>My Personality Quirks and Foibles</u>

Much of the reason why I fish in the ways that I do is because my own personality quirks, foibles, and my likes and dislikes. I recognize that this limits my fishing options and makes me more than a little quirky and opinionated. But I don't care – this is how I shape my own fishing comfort zone (and after all, that is the subject of this book).

- I am an impatient person and do not want to fish in ways that take a great deal of preparation or rigging time.

- I have a relatively short attention span that keeps me from choosing long fishing trips on a regular basis. That includes avoiding long drives to get to the launch, long boat rides once in the water, and extended time on the water. Being semi-retired, with a very flexible schedule, I can fish often and prefer half-day trips when I go. I typically fish 3 to 5 days a week year round, and rarely do my door-to-door trip times exceed 6 hours.

- I do not like fishing trips in the dark (before dawn or after dusk). I am uncomfortable navigating in the dark, and do not like launching, retrieving, and unloading at home in the dark. I do make exceptions to this if I am fishing on someone else's boat.

- I am not a creative artisan nor am I good at making my own lures. Many anglers are quite talented and get great enjoyment from making attractive lures and flies and then catching fish on their own creations. I wish I had that talent, but sadly I do not.

- I do not like treble hooks or multiple hooks on a lure. I find that treble hooks are more damaging to the fish, and offer greater potential for me to get a hook stuck in a body part. That is a big reason that I own and throw very few hard-plastic plugs and lures. When I do use that type of lure, I generally cut off one or two of the prongs on the treble hook and crimp down the barbs on the remaining hook(s). Or I may replace a treble hook with a plain J-hook or a J-hook with bucktail tied on. There is a negative feedback system involved here – I don't like treble-hooked lures, so I don't throw them often. I don't take time to fish those lures well, and my catches using those lures are not good.

- I am very comfortable with spinning reels, but do not like revolving spool reels (baitcasters and trolling reels). I do not fly fish for various reasons, so I don't use fly reels either.

- I prefer fishing in saltwater. I live in an area with close access to water with low to medium salinity. Most of my out-of-town fishing trips are made to areas with full marine salinity. Less than 5% of my fishing is done in freshwater.

- Over the years I often fished by myself and did not want to own a large boat and towing vehicle that had high operating, maintenance, and storage costs and nobody to share expenses for many of the trips. In recent years, I have enjoyed fishing with other anglers from kayaks – we each have our own boats and tackle and are responsible for our own catching success or failure.

- I do not like cleaning fish, and neither my wife nor I are creative at cooking fish. As a result I rarely bring fish home. I bring a few fish home when on chartered trips or when fishing from my center console, but do not bring home fish caught on my kayak.

- I try to keep competition out of my fishing. I have entered a few low-key tournaments over the years and had several wins (most notably winning all or parts of the Severn River Rod and Keg Club's winter pickerel derby several years in a row) along with many non-wins. During 2015, I made a decision that I was through with tournaments and would no longer participate. That decision (like all other aspects of my fishing comfort zone) is subject to reconsideration as time goes on.

- I don't like anchoring my boat. Over the years I have avoided anchoring unless it was absolutely necessary. I preferred fishing while drifting. When fishing from my kayaks in Maryland I almost never use an anchor. When I fish in shallow flats in Florida, an anchor becomes an important part of the gear.

Key Criteria

Having explained the personality traits that shape my fishing preferences, here are several key criteria that I try to follow. Much of my decision-making process involves a mental comparison of the cost (in money, time, space, aggravation) of an activity vs. the benefit to me (increased catching, larger fish, etc.).

1. Keep Things Simple: If I have a choice between a complicated rigging technique and one that is considerable simpler, I usually choose the simpler one. The complicated technique may offer some incrementally higher probability of catching fish, but the cost and/or hassle of following the complicated technique is usually not worth the benefit to me. For example, some anglers feel strongly that dipping their lures in scented fluids that can add contrasting colors and aroma to the lure will trigger more bites. The lures shown below were purchased at a winter flea market several years ago from one of the more successful light tackle jiggers in the Chesapeake Bay region. He and his fishing buddies used these actual lures during the previous season. They had excellent success with those lures. What is unclear to me is how much of the success came from the tweaked lures and how much was the result of their personal skills honed over dozens of trips and hundreds of hours spent jigging.

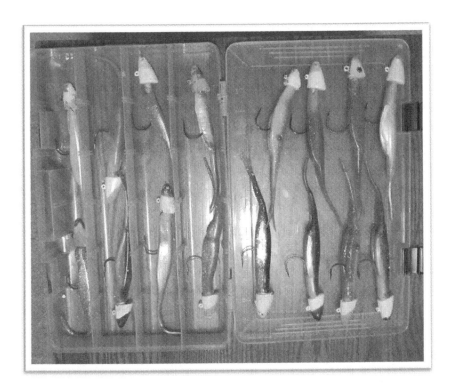

Proponents of lure tweaking and modification may be right – but doing so adds complexity, cost, and preparation time. If you enjoy the lure tweaking and believe you are improving your odds then go for it – those efforts are within your fishing comfort zone. But I have pretty good success with untweaked lures – and that is my comfort zone.

Some anglers change lures frequently. I tend to stick with the same lure for an extended time unless I can observe that other lure types are performing better. I spend more time fishing, and less time getting new lures out of their storage boxes and tying them on. If you fish with leaders and tie on new lures often, you quickly use up the leader and need to stop to add a new leader.

I prefer using a small number of rods and reels with similar features and a small number of lures in which I have high confidence rather than buying many different rods, reels, and lures. My entire current stable of rods includes 12 spinning rods. When fishing with light tackle guides in Maryland and Florida, I use similar types of spinning tackle. For 2015, I caught 38 species of fish (including 4 that were new for me) and had 9 personal bests in terms of fish length. That is not bad for a limited choice of rods. Nearly all those fish were caught on just a few simple types of lures (jighead with paddletail or twister tail, jighead with live minnow, and small safety pin-style spinnerbaits). I will speak more about these in later chapters.

2. Avoid Clutter: Most of my fishing using watercraft has been done in small boats or kayaks that offer limited storage space. Even my largest boat, a 23' center console, did not have numerous large built-in storage bins like some other boats offer. I learned early on that keeping tackle and gear organized and having a designated place for everything I bring aboard is a great timesaver. I am a strong believer in bringing only as many rods with you as you can store and control easily. To help with that, I added extra rod holders on all my vessels. My small center console boat is equipped with 14 rod holders. I have four adjustable rod holders on my kayaks.

I also discovered that most of the time I used only a small percentage of all the tackle I had on board for any given trip. Once I reached the decision to limit myself to a small amount of tackle for each trip, gear storage became much easier. Today in my kayak fishing trips I bring one or two waterproof Plano trays and sometimes a small liquid bait container (for Gulp baits) that hold all the gear I need for a day's trip. They are stored easily out of the way. In the photo below, the small plastic tray holding the jigheads fits inside the larger waterproof tray, which holds soft plastics, a Leatherman tool, some basic first aid supplies, some tools for repairing kayak components, and my fishing license. If I am planning to use more than one style of fishing during the trip (e.g., casting for perch, trolling for stripers, jigging deep water for stripers) I may bring a second waterproof tray like the one shown in the lower right.

On my 16' center console boat, I have the storage space to carry a few more trays but I really don't need as much tackle as I bring.

Many kayak anglers worry about losing rods, tools, and other tackle overboard. Often they use leashes to secure their gear to the kayak hull or attach floats. These measures do provide better security but they introduce many ropes or cords into the working cockpit area or add bulky foam floats to rods. I know that I would be very frustrated by snagging leashes with hooks or by bumping into the foam flotation on rods. As a result, I do not use leashes or floats. I accept the potential of losing a piece of gear occasionally (the cost) in exchange for avoiding annoying leashes and floats (the benefit).

Storing tackle at home can benefit from good planning and an orderly storage system. I tried various methods for storing my rods and reels. I used several approaches that held the rods horizontally on a wall or on storage arms. They were good in theory, but I had a hard time pulling out individual rods.

After some trial and error, I installed three 4-slot rod holders on the garage wall to keep the rods in a vertical position. I also built a set of wooden storage shelves in the garage to hold all my other tackle. It is easy to find what I want.

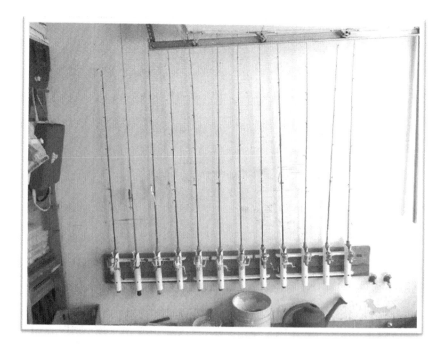

3. Look for Launch Spots That are Close to Home and Close to the Fishing Grounds

I noted previously that I do not like long drives to get to the launch, nor do I like long boat rides. Sometimes this cannot be avoided to get to places that hold the fish you want to target. But in my fishing life, those trips are minimized. During 2015, I made more than 100 fishing trips. Here are some rough statistics for those trips.

- On about 50% of my trips I launched my kayaks from one of two ramps in the Severn River near Annapolis. Both of these are located less than 15 minutes from my home.

  The launch location I use most often is the Tucker Street launch. It is only 10 minutes from my home. The photo shows an extremely low water level that day – usually only a few feet of the beach is exposed.

I also launch often from the beach at Jonas Green State Park which is 15 minutes from my home.

Photo Credit: Mark Bange

- Another 20% of the trips were made in my kayaks or my center console to Eastern Bay and the creeks and bays of Kent Island. The launch spots I used for these trips are located from 25 to 40 minutes from home.

- 10% of the trips (all in the center console) launched from Sandy Point State Park located 15-20 minutes from my home for fishing in the main Chesapeake Bay.

- Another 15% of the trips were made in Florida with a kayak fishing guide. The drive time from my hotel to the launch points ranged from 15 to 40 minutes. I do acknowledge that there was extensive travel time to get from Maryland to Florida, but once there, I stayed for several days each time and was close to the action.

- The remaining small percentage of trips went to a variety of locations, both freshwater and saltwater. Some trips involved long drives. In isolated instances, it is well worth it to me to travel long ways to get to fishing opportunities that are not available for me locally. But for my day-to-day fishing, I prefer to spend more time fishing and less time getting there.

In nearly all of these cases I was able to begin fishing within a few minutes after launching.

4. Gain Familiarity with a Few Areas that Are Your "Home Waters"

I have several locations that I have fished repeatedly throughout the year and for multiple years. Through this iterative process, I have come to get a better sense of the fish patterns within my home waters. First and foremost of these is the Severn River near my home in Annapolis. I estimate that in recent years I have been on the river and its tidal creeks and ponds at least 75 times each year. Nearly all those trips have been in a kayak, which limits my travel range, but allows me to be in closer contact to the water, move more slowly than in a power boat, and creep quietly into skinny-water locations where fish often reside.

The photo shows a local spot that often produces stripers while trolling in the river. Before posting the photo on local fishing boards, I intentionally blocked out the background to disguise the location. One of my buddies named this spot "The Fog Bank" for obvious reasons.

Photo Credit: Mark Bange

Another area that is becoming home waters to me is the eastern shoreline of Kent Island, the Kent Narrows, and other shallow water locations around the edges of Eastern Bay. I found that during 2015, I spent many mornings and a few afternoons exploring, looking for fish, bait, and other wildlife around Eastern Bay. In my kayak, I focus on shallow water (usually 3' to 6') along edges. I watch the fishfinder and GPS chartplotter on my kayak and make mental notes of where I catch fish and how that shifts throughout the year. In my center console, I am able to cover more ground and explore places too remote to reach in my kayak. Each year I learn a few new spots that have strong potential for holding fish. Those fish are not there on every trip, but by knowing those spots, and checking them periodically, I get a better sense of when and where to expect fish.

After fishing 20 days in the Tampa Bay region during 2015, I like to think that these areas are becoming "adopted" home waters. I will never know them as well as local anglers do, but I am learning how to fish there and what things to look for to improve my chances.

Each angler has a limited amount of hours, days, and years to fish. In my earlier years, I spent a lot of time exploring new areas, often with limited success. As time went along, I realized that I wanted to improve my knowledge and skills. I believe that by focusing on a few key home water locations an angler can grow far more skilled in catching fish there. On those few occasions when I venture to new locations, I can call on what I learned in my home waters for clues on how to fish, and which sections of the new water bodies offer me the best opportunities.

This book does not go into detail on specific fishing spots. Lenny Rudow offers a remarkable amount of detailed location information in his "Rudow's Guide to Fishing the Chesapeake". Readers are referred to that book for suggestions on where to look for fish, as well of descriptions on different fishing methods.

5. Make Fishing Decisions Based on What You Like, Not on What You Are Told to Do

There is great temptation for inexperienced anglers to pattern themselves after more experienced anglers. These could be family members, friends, guides, or experts who they heard speak at a seminar or whose blog they read. This is logical -- however, blindly following others, without understanding why they do something and what all is involved, is not always productive. If I tried to fish only using the methods I read about from others or saw others using, I would be confused, and probably frustrated by using equipment and methods that are not necessarily right for me.

For example, when I bought my first 17' boat, I had heard various speakers and read articles about trolling with heavy tackle. That seemed like the best way to fish. I bought several trolling rod and reel combos and lures recommended by others and spent some time trying them out. I did not have enough knowledge to do it well, nor was I willing to try trip-after-trip to refine my methods. Eventually I lost all interest in trolling with heavy tackle, and I sold that type of equipment.

Those experiences were not fruitless, however. I found that when I was out chasing diving birds and breaking fish and casting light lures with spinning tackle, often the fish stopped biting and the birds moved away as soon as a boat approached. Those fish had not left the area, but I could not tell where they had gone. I discovered that I could troll slowly with the same light rods and small lures I was casting around an area and eventually I could get a few bites and learn where the fish had moved. At that point I could continue trolling or could stop and cast to them.

My trolling interest evolved further as I spent more time fishing from kayaks. I found that I could troll small lures using light spinning tackle and catch many fish. Over the past 4 years, I spent a growing percentage of my fishing time trolling from my kayaks and was able to see a noticeable increase in my catching success, both in the total number of fish and in the size of the fish.

19

This example shows that trolling as a fishing technique is not inherently bad, but it may not be suited to each angler. By modifying techniques based on hands-on trial and error, I was able to adapt trolling to a format that worked for me and was highly enjoyable. I moved trolling from outside to inside my comfort zone, but it took more than a decade and lots of practice to get there.

You often hear someone say that lure XYZ is the best thing out there. You may purchase that lure in different sizes and colors and try to use it. You may find that your experience with that lure is far less productive than the results espoused by the person who told you to use it. It is possible that the person had a vested financial interest in getting you to buy that product. Or they could have taken the time to learn how to work that lure to get the best reaction from the fish. If you do not have that knowledge, you are unlikely to duplicate the other person's success.

Buying new equipment is fun, but it can become an expensive hobby. I know many anglers who have many hundreds (or thousands) of dollars of unused tackle sitting in their homes. They keep telling themselves that they will eventually get around to using that lure or learning how to make great catches with that product.

The tackle selection portion of my fishing comfort zone has narrowed over the years as I have tried different types of rods, reels, and lures and realized that I liked some products and disliked others. These days I am rather selective in buying new products. Unless I feel confident that a new lure will out-produce the ones I already have, or if someone gives me the new lure for free to try out, I tend to stick with the tried and true products. As an example, most of my rods are the same brand and all of my reels are the same model in different sizes. My lure collection is relatively uniform compared to the wide variety of styles and colors found in most other angler's tackle boxes.

Chapter 3 - My Fishing Evolution

The Early Years

I grew up in a small town in eastern Pennsylvania that had a trout stream running through it. I occasionally went to the stream using a child's rod and reel and some worms I dug up in the backyard. I never caught a single trout there, and quickly lost interest. My father was not a fisherman, and I had no older brothers, cousins, or close friends who were anglers and could show me how to catch trout. As a result, even though good fishing was nearby, it played a very small part of my boyhood experiences. Clearly trout fishing was not in my boyhood comfort zone.

I did have somewhat better fishing success when once each summer the neighbor who lived next door to us would take my younger brother and me to his country farm, which had a pond stocked with bluegills. We could float pieces of earthworms under a bobber and catch one bluegill (or sunny, as we called them) after another. I recall one time when we ran out of worms, I pulled a few squashed bugs off the radiator in the car, and we kept catching sunnies for another half hour.

After those limited Pennsylvania fishing experiences in my younger years, I did not fish again until I was in my 30s and living in Maryland. A close friend enjoyed fishing and took me with him in his canoe on some freshwater ponds. I caught a few fish and decided I could spring for my own rod and reel and a handful of tackle. We continued fishing from time to time and soon I realized that I enjoyed fishing, but preferred saltwater to freshwater.

Getting on the Water

I bought my first boat in 1987 (a 13 foot Gheenoe with a 4-hp outboard).

I had fun messing around[2], crabbing, and even caught a few fish by bottom fishing with squid strips and bloodworms. A few years later my family moved to Annapolis, MD. I bought and sold a series of small boats over the next 10 years and spent more time fishing in the mid-Chesapeake Bay region.

- 10' jon boat
- 13' Boston Whaler
- 14' aluminum V-hull skiff
- 17' Boston Whaler Montauk
- 11' Avon inflatable
- 17' Scout 172 Sportfish.

My fishing was not very sophisticated – I did mostly bottom fishing and casting to breaking fish. I caught plenty of fish, but they were generally small. Nevertheless I enjoyed the experience.

---

[2] This brings to mind a famous quote from Wind in the Willows by Kenneth Grahame: "There is nothing — absolutely nothing — half so much worth doing as simply messing about in boats."

Over those years I got a taste of offshore fishing from several charter trips booked at Cape Hatteras and from fishing with members of the Annapolis Chapter of the MSSA out of Wachapreague, VA. These were great opportunities to fish far from shore with the potential to catch big game species. I enjoyed these trips and caught tuna, wahoo, dolphin, and other species, but soon realized that the cost and time involved to fish offshore were not something I really enjoyed -- offshore fishing moved outside of my fishing comfort zone.

Nearer to home I made a few charter trips trolling for stripers and bluefish in the Chesapeake Bay. I found that I did not enjoy traditional trolling, with very heavy rods and large revolving spool reels. When a fish hit the lure it was fun for a few minutes, but the rest of the time was often monotonous for me. This style of fishing, while quite effective, was also outside my comfort zone.

On one of my trips to Cape Hatteras, I met Doug Martin, a fishing guide in Hatteras, NC, who introduced me to the pleasures of catching a variety of game fish using light spinning tackle. I realized that this style of fishing was something I enjoyed and could do at home too. After that, my charter dollars were mainly spent on guides who could offer light tackle fishing opportunities.

Six-Foot-itis

As my enthusiasm for fishing expanded my desire to have a larger boat increased too. I recall attending a January 2002 fishing and boat show in Timonium, MD. My goal was to look at 20' to 21' center console boats as an upgrade from my 17' foot Scout. I visited Tri-State Marine's booth and saw a sweet 2001 Parker 23 SE center console that had been used the previous season by light tackle guide Richie Gaines. The boat was being offered at a price I could afford and came with a new-boat warranty. I had fished with Richie previously and liked his boat, so I made an impulse buy and jumped up six feet in boat length. I thoroughly enjoyed having a larger boat that could take more pounding than my body could and still get home safely. I also liked the ability to take larger groups of family and friends out for fishing or sightseeing rides.

Photo Credit: Marian Higgins

With that boat, named "Hate to Wait" (a reflection of my impatient nature) I fished many times each year and could cover more ground. A friend offered me storage on a boat lift at her home on the South River. From that home base I explored waters from the Chester River to the Choptank River. Nearly all my fishing was light tackle casting, running-and-gunning to breaking fish, and bottom fishing.

Downsizing

By the 2008 season, I realized that I no longer needed a boat as large and heavy as the Parker. I could not store a boat on a trailer in my yard due to homeowner's association rules, and I did not own a vehicle powerful enough to tow the heavy Parker anyway. I sold the Parker in September 2008 and began looking for the largest boat that I could fit in my garage. That fall, I bought a used 15' Gheenoe and added a 9.9-hp motor. Over the winter I outfitted the boat with electronics, better seating and other features with the goal of making it more fishable.

Once I got it on the water the following spring, I realized that the Gheenoe was not the boat I wanted for my fishing comfort zone. It did not have sufficient speed or freeboard to allow me to travel long distances over open water to get to the places I wanted to fish. While I still needed a boat that would fit into my garage, I needed a more seaworthy vessel. I also wanted to be able to take other anglers with me when I fished.

I spent several months studying small center consoles for their seaworthiness and fishability. I found a 2000 Scout 162 Sportfish with a 70-hp motor. It could just fit in into my garage when turned at an angle, and I could tow it with my 6-cylinder van. It had not been well cared for and took some time to restore the appearance and repair some mechanical and electrical items. I added electronics and a bow-mounted trolling motor and soon fell in love with the new boat. I learned that I could move easily in waves up to 2 feet. Beyond that the ride became wet and bouncy. The boat operated with the gas motor in depths down to about 18" and even shallower with the trolling motor I added later. The boat offered flat platforms on both the bow and stern with provisions to add an elevated seat in each location. It is a very stable platform for the light tackle fishing I enjoy.

Photo Credit: Woody Tillery

Because of its small size and nimbleness, I named the Scout "Small but Perky". I use it to chase breaking fish under birds, look for fish on the sonar and jig on them, and to move slowly and stealthily in marsh guts, shallow flats, sod bank edges, and stump fields to cast to fish. The only tackle I carry on the Scout is light to medium-heavy spinning rods used for casting, jigging, and occasionally trolling to find where the fish are. These light tackle techniques are a major part of my current fishing comfort zone.

At some point during those years I learned of a fishing technique called light tackle jigging or LTJ. It allows the angler to use medium to medium-heavy rods with weighted lures and still catch large fish. I liked the concept because the angler is in constant contact with the line and can feel even the smallest tap or bite.

I tried this on my own boat and booked several charters with light tackle guides like Richie Gaines and Walleye Pete Dahlberg. I learned the basics of the technique but never mastered it the way that other anglers did. Local fishing author Shawn Kimbro is a leading practitioner of LTJ. He and his group of fishing buddies are highly successful at finding large striped bass that they catch using LTJ methods. They are in their fishing comfort zone. For me, having an LTJ comfort zone is something I aspire to, but I have not yet reached that goal.

<u>Fishing from Kayaks</u>

I use my center console boats from May through November. I wanted to find another type of watercraft that I could use during the winter months and on days when I did not want to deal with the logistics of trailering a boat to a launch point. I find that on windy or rough days I tend to use the kayak more than the Scout because I can tuck the kayak into tidal creeks and coves that offer some wind protection.

I bought my first sit-on-top kayak in 2001 – an Ocean Kayak Drifter. I used it for paddling trips and occasionally would bring some rods with me for casting small lures for white perch or pickerel. I found that I really enjoyed fishing from a kayak, but recognized that the Drifter did not offer a dry or comfortable sitting position.

In 2008 I booked my first kayak fishing charter with guide Cory Routh in Virginia Beach, VA. I had been on a multi-year quest to catch a redfish. I booked trips with guides in Florida, Texas, and Louisiana and never was able to catch one. I was excited and relieved when Cory found redfish for me — I caught seven of them during a 4-hour trip. Cory provided a kayak for me to use. It was a Native Watercraft Manta Ray 14. I was amazed at how much more comfortable the seating was on the Manta Ray compared to my Drifter. That fall I bought a Manta Ray of my own.

I found that the logistics and costs of fishing from my kayak were preferable to towing a boat to a launch ramp and paying for the fuel and other expenses. I could drive 10-15 minutes from my home, launch a kayak quickly, and begin fishing. Each year after that I seemed to make more fishing trips in my kayaks than I did in my center consoles. I still loved having a boat for trips that covered more ground, but the kayak offered other benefits, like being able to sneak up on fish and giving me a workout while I enjoyed my fishing.

As I grew fonder of kayak fishing, I decided to apply to become a member of Native Watercraft's Pro Staff team. I joined the team in 2012. I have owned several Native kayaks – I currently own two Native kayaks - a pedal-drive Slayer Propel model in 10' length, and an 11' Manta Ray paddle kayak.

In January 2013, through an internet search, I found Tampa, FL kayak fishing guide Neil Taylor of Strike Three Kayak Fishing and booked a trip. I quickly found that he and I had very similar fishing styles, philosophies, conservation ethics, and fishing comfort zones – we became friends. I booked several more trips in 2013 and 2014 then made six trips (for 20 days of fishing) during 2015.

While Tampa is far from Maryland, I can get there easily in a two-hour flight and can fish from a kayak for warm-water game species. Neil fishes with light tackle and usually in shallow water. The lessons I learned from fishing with him helped my fishing success at home too. The photo shows several of our group at the end of a February 2016 trip on a cold and windy day. The kayak I used is in the foreground, and Neil is the person on the right.

Photo Credit: John Rentch

These days, a large percentage of my fishing time is spent in kayaks. It truly is a large part of my fishing comfort zone. Later chapters in this book talk about kayak fishing, how to choose a kayak for fishing, and what accessories are useful for kayak fishing.

Other Noteworthy Fishing Experiences

Fifteen years ago, I went on a multi-year quest to catch my first tarpon. I found a guide in Florida who specialized in tarpon fishing. It took several

trips to finally find good weather conditions and feeding tarpon. In May 2003, my fishing buddy Mike Paque from Oklahoma and I each caught several tarpon heavier than 100 pounds with the largest at 170 pounds at Boca Grande, FL. My first tarpon ever caught is shown in the photo. The captain was very intense in his desire to find tarpon. It added some stress to the trip. Although it was exciting to hook and fight several tarpon, I am unlikely to make trips focused solely on tarpon again – that has moved outside of my fishing comfort zone.

On a business trip to Aberdeen, Scotland in 2006, I met up with a friend, Jon Getliff, who took me to fly fish in a for-pay stocked trout lake and let me use one of his fly rods.

I had never tried a fly rod before. Jon caught two trout. I stood on the edge of the pond and would watch the huge trout swim slowly past my fly and never show any interest. Despite my failure to catch a fish on the fly rod, it gave me a sense of the great trout fishing tradition in Scotland.

Doug Dixon, a friend whom I met while working on cooling water issues at power plants, has a Ph.D. in fisheries biology and is an avid and adventuresome angler. He invited me on several fishing trips to places I would not have gone on my own. Twice we traveled to remote Lake Nahmakanta in the north woods of Maine (2007 and 2008). We stayed in a cabin and fished the main lake as well as in several small ponds to which we hiked in. The camp owner had stationed canoes and rowboats at each pond for his clients to use. I caught mainly small land-locked Atlantic salmon and brook trout on ultralight tackle. The photo shows Doug with a fish caught in the main lake.

Another time Doug set up a trip to troll for salmon and trout in Lake Michigan. I caught the two largest fish that day (beginner's luck, I guess).

In 2011, Doug organized a four-day trip out of Homer, AK. Our group of six anglers chartered a 52' boat where we lived for the entire trip.

We caught our limit of halibut each day and found several other species I had never seen before, like the ling cod, black rockfish, and yellow eye rockfish.

Last, but not least, was my first ice-fishing trip – made at a pond in western Maryland. My mentor for pickerel fishing, Virgil Poe, also has a passion for ice fishing. In January 2010, he invited me to join him. Virgil had all the gear we needed as he drilled a series of holes in the ice. We fished several tip-ups and also jigged with maggots. It was a successful day as we caught bluegills, yellow perch, largemouth bass, and a warmouth.

These were wonderful experiences to see different habitats, use different techniques, and to catch fish of many species I did not find in my home waters. I am thankful to have had these opportunities, but I do not have a strong desire to return to fish in those locations and in those ways again. My fishing experience was enriched by those opportunities, but the same experiences helped to shape my current fishing comfort zone.

A Special Year

I had a noteworthy year in 2012 for several reasons. I had been retired for a full year and was beginning to see improvements in catching success as a result of being on the water many more days in 2011.

In 2010 and 2011 I set a goal for myself to catch at least one fish per month. I fished somewhat during the winter, but both years I missed catching a fish during one of the winter months. In 2012 I set the same goal. The winter was mild and allowed me to fish frequently. I had no trouble getting my fish for January and February. At some point during March, I looked back at my records and saw that I had caught at least one fish each calendar week to that point. After some hesitation, I reset my goal to catch a fish each week. Although I had frequent out-of-town travel and had to work around weather conditions and family commitments, I reached the end of December with my weekly record still intact. The final week of the year was a short one – it included just December 30 and 31. I ventured out on a day with wet snow falling and soon caught a pickerel. My record was intact! I immediately discontinued any organized effort to catch a weekly fish.

During that noteworthy year, I had one other remarkable fishing experience. I talk more about this in a later chapter. But because of a fish I caught on January 1, 2012, I ended up winning the grand prize in the year-long Maryland Fishing Challenge.

Part Two: Fishing Gear

Chapter 4 – Rods and Reels and My Comfort Zone

In this chapter I talk about rods and reels of different types. I tend to have a pretty narrow focus on rod and reel type in my fishing comfort zone – I use only spinning tackle. As a result, I do not have much experience using revolving spool reels such as trolling reels or baitcasters. I have owned several reels of those types and also have used them on charter boats. As my fishing comfort zone evolved, I realized I did not enjoy using those types of reels and sold them. I tried fly fishing twice without success using rods provided by friends and never felt any interest in continuing fishing with that type of tackle or to purchase my own fly rod.

I provide discussion about all those types of gear but I primarily describe spinning tackle. At the end of this chapter I explain the types of rods and reels I use and how I rig them.

Given my lack of long-term personal experience with rods and reels other than spinning tackle, I cannot do a thorough review of the merits of types of equipment other than what I use. This type of comparative information can be found in other fishing books. The fishing books by Shawn Kimbro and Alan Battista that I referenced previously offer their perspectives on rod and reel choices. Their preferred rod and reel selections overlap with my personal choice somewhat, but there are many differences. That is part of finding a personal fishing comfort zone. Readers are encouraged to review those other books to get more information on rod and reel choice.

Spinning Reels

Spinning reels are easy to use and often serve as starting reels for beginners. They range in size from tiny ultralight reels to large, heavy reels used for big-game fishing. The cost of spinning reels covers a range of less than $10 to more than $1,000 for a single reel. Each major reel manufacturer offers different product lines and different sizes. The sizes are often expressed in "thousands", such as 1000, 2500, 3000, etc. The largest size reel I found in a quick internet search was a Shimano Stella 20000 reel that weighs nearly two pounds and costs $1,259 at retail. The smallest size I generally see is a 1000 series reel that weighs only a few ounces. I have seen 500 series reels in catalogs, but have never used one.

Larger reels can hold more line, and typically can handle line with higher test ratings. Reels designed for saltwater use generally have more corrosion-resistant metal alloys used in their construction. Better reels tend to have more bearings and higher quality bearings. The better reels also offer anti-reverse (the handle does not rotate at all in the reverse direction) as you make a hook set or lift the rod tip while jigging. Each angler must find their comfort zone on what they are willing to pay for a reel after considering the type of fishing they plan to do and their budget.

The reel shown in the next photo is a Shimano Stradic 3000 series reel. It is designed for saltwater use and offers anti-reverse, fast gear ratio, and a lubrication port on the reel body.

Spinning reels have a fixed spool and an arm that spins around the longitudinal axis of the rod. On a cast the line runs off the top of the spool to move out through the guides along the length of the rod. A curved wire on the front of the arm (the bail) collects line after a cast allowing it to wrap onto the spool. To make a cast, the angler opens the bail, holds the line with a finger, and flips the rod forward. The finger is released at the right moment, allowing the line to run off the spool. Once the lure or bait hits the water, the angler closes the bail either by cranking the handle or by manually flipping the bail closed. Most beginners use the handle-turning

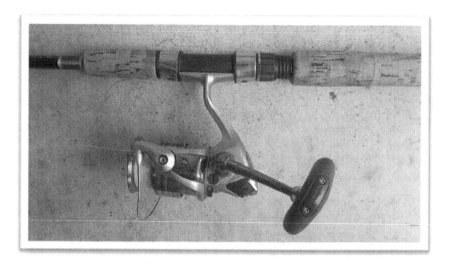

method. More experienced anglers close the bail manually to avoid getting loops in the line

Spinning reels are generally used with the reel hanging below the rod and the handle on the left side. Most spinning reels are designed to allow the handle to be moved easily to the right side for left-handed anglers. I have occasionally seen inexperienced anglers turn the rod upside down so that the reel is above the rod. This puts the handle on the opposite side and requires the user to turn the handle in a backwards direction.

Spinning reels come with adjustable drag systems that offer resistance when a fish pulls against the line. Most spinning reel drags are located at the front end of the spool. A disk can be rotated to increase or decrease the amount of drag resistance. Some spinning reels have the drag knob on the rear of the body of the reel. I personally prefer the drag in the front.

A few spinning reel models are designed with dual drag systems – one in the front and a second lighter drag in the rear. This style reel is most often used when livelining with bait. The main drag can be set tight enough to control a large fish. The rear drag is set with enough resistance to allow the bait to swim, but not enough to free spool the reel fully. Once a fish takes the bait, the angler can close the rear drag lever or begin turning the handle.

Different models of spinning reels offer different gear ratios. For example a reel with a 4:1 ratio will rotate the arm and collect line four times for each full rotation of the handle. A reel with a 6:1 ratio will collect line six times for each handle rotation. A higher gear ratio offers faster lure movement, whereas a lower gear ratio allows more cranking power.

Spinning Rods

Spinning rods come in different lengths, generally from about 5' for ultralight rods, to monsters longer than 10' for surf casting. Most rods today are made from graphite, although some are made of fiberglass or a blend of graphite and fiberglass. Spinning rods range in cost from under $10 to hundreds of dollars for a custom-built rod using high-quality components -- often custom rods are decorated with detailed designs that make them works of art.

Spinning rods have a handle (typically covered with cork or foam), a reel seat where the mounting bracket on the reel is attached to the rod, and the rest of the rod that has a series of rings (guides) attached at intervals out to the rod tip. The guides channel the line from the reel spool to the tip of the rod. They are spaced to aid in casting and to let the angler use the strength and flexibility of the full length of the rod when fighting a large fish.

I can share a story here about the importance of passing the line through all the guides. I booked two days of tarpon fishing in 2003. After the first day, the captain told the mate to respool the reel with fresh line. He did so, but forgot to thread the line through the first (largest diameter) rod guide. I was using that rod when I hooked a tarpon estimated at 170 pounds. I fought the fish for 20 minutes before noticing that only the outer half of the rod was bending as I applied pressure on the fish. For a fish that size, I was unable to take advantage of the bending strength of the full rod because of the bypassed guide. What should have been a 10-15 minute fight took 45 minutes as I moved the fish to within 10 feet of the boat multiple times, then the fish surged and swam out again.

The handle sections on some spinning rods have split grips (smaller sections of grip at the ends of the handle region with the middle section showing the exposed rod blank. Some anglers prefer this style because they believe they can more easily feel vibrations through the exposed section.

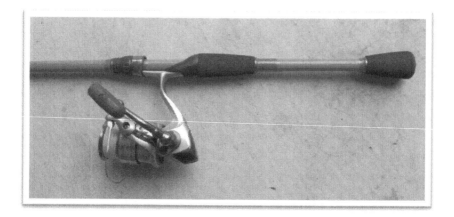

The length of the handle section behind the reel seat is variable. I have one 6' ultralight rod that has a very short handle section behind the reel seat.

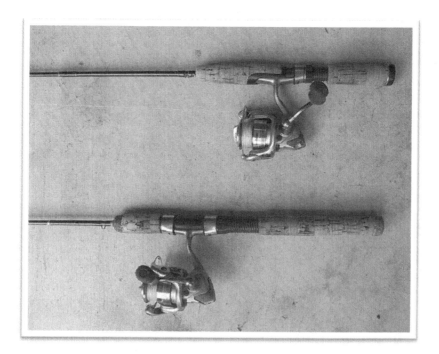

The photo shows two 6' ultralight rods – the total rod length is identical. The one with the short handle has an additional 4" of working length beyond the reel seat, effectively making the rod perform like a 6'4" rod in a 6' length.

I bought that rod as an impulse buy at a winter tackle show. I picked it up and saw that the rod had a decal advertising "Carbon Veil" technology. I figured I would probably never again see a rod with my last name on it – I bought it on the spot. Initially I found the short handle a bit awkward. But after I got used to it, it has become my favorite ultralight rod. Even though it is a slender rod, it has tamed pickerel to 24", hundreds of white perch, and striped bass to 19".

Spinning rods are designed using two criteria – power and action.

- Power refers to the general strength and bend-resistance of the rod. Most rods are designed with ultralight, light, medium-light, medium, medium-heavy, or heavy power. Some are available in extra-heavy power.

- Action refers to how the rod bends when put under load. Action is usually expressed as slow, medium, fast, or extra-fast. A fast action rod bends mainly in the outer end, whereas a slow action rod bends throughout most of its length. A slow action provides more whip for casting light lures. A fast action gives better hooksets when jigging.

Spinning rods typically are made in one-piece and two-piece versions. Most anglers feel that a one-piece rod offers better sensitivity. If you have challenges in transporting or storing a one-piece rod, you may prefer getting a two-piece rod. Prior to 2003, I drove a 4-door sedan. I could not easily fit 6'6" or 7' rods inside. All the rods I bought in those days were two-piece. After 2003, I drove a van that could easily accommodate one-piece rods. All the rods I bought since then are one-piece.

If you plan to carry a fishing rod on an airplane, you can buy large rod cases to hold long one-piece rods. These will be checked luggage. You can also buy travel rods that break down into 3 or more sections and are stowed in a tube less than 3' long. These travel rods can be brought onboard as carry-on luggage. The rod pictured below is a 7' St. Croix Premier medium power rod. I used it to catch fish in Florida, Texas, and Alaska while on trips to those states.

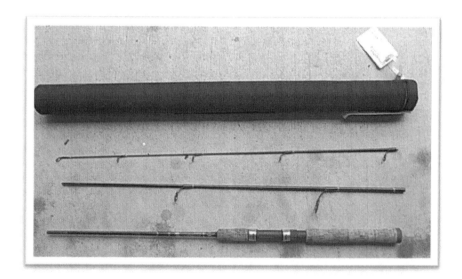

Baitcasting Rods and Reels

Having described spinning tackle in some detail, I move on to other common types of rods and reels. In the next few sections, I offer brief overviews on baitcasting, trolling, and fly fishing rods and reels. I do not own or use any of these types of rods and reels now and do not follow the technological innovations in this style of tackle. The photos of baitcasting and trolling equipment were taken at a local outdoors store using rods and reels they had on display.

Like spinning reels, baitcasting reels or baitcasters come in different sizes and are made of different materials. Costs vary widely. The spool on a baitcaster rotates on an axis perpendicular to the rod axis. The line pulls off the face of the spool rather than off the top of the spool (as in a spinning reel). This generates less line twist. Most baitcasters have a "level-wind" mechanism that spreads line evenly across the face of the spool as the line is retrieved.

Baitcasters are very popular – many anglers believe they offer better casting accuracy and easier line control for jigging when compared to spinning equipment. But the casting method when using a baitcaster creates potential for the spool to keep spinning after the lure hits the water leading to a backlash or "birds nest" of tangled line. Regular baitcaster users have educated their thumbs to "feather" the spool during the cast and to stop it from spinning at just the right moment when the lure hits the water. With experience they do this automatically and do not think about it. Also modern baitcaster technology helps to minimize the potential for backlashes with the use of adjustable magnetic spool controls. A magnetic control setting on the reel allows users to adjust the spool's resistance during the cast so that it is appropriate for the weight of the lure and wind conditions present.

Baitcasting reels, like spinning reels, are made with different gear ratios. Higher ratios allow users to rip spinner baits at fast speeds through the water while the lower ratios are appropriate for keeping big lipped crankbaits moving in deep water at the proper depth.

In general, baitcasters are designed to cast heavier lures than spinning reels. There are always exceptions, but rarely are baitcasters used for lures weighing 1/8 oz. or less. While such lures work great on medium and light spinning reels, they would pose a challenge to most baitcasting reels.

The photos below show two styles of baitcasting reels. The first photo shows a conventional round-bodied reel. The second photo shows a "low-profile" reel. Generally the round-bodied style has a larger spool allowing more line capacity. The low-profile design may fit more comfortably in the hands of some anglers who like to have constant contact with the line.

Unlike most spinning reels, the handles on baitcasters are placed on the right hand side of the reel body. Some anglers prefer to have the handle on the left side of the body – left-handed versions of many baitcasting reels are available. The five-pointed "star" drags are seen between the reel body and handle. They can be loosened or tightened to adjust the drag.

The next photo shows a top view of a baitcaster. The spool runs horizontally across the reel. The bar in front of the spool holds the level-wind mechanism. The light-colored piece behind the spool is the line release button that is depressed before casting to allow free spinning movement of the spool. Once the lure lands, the handle is turned, which closes the line-release button.

Baitcasting rods are designed in much the same manner as the spinning rods described previously. They come in different lengths, power, and action and have a wide range of prices.

There are two main differences between a baitcasting rod and a spinning rod – the way the rod is held and the trigger grip on the handle. Baitcasting gear is fished with the reel on top of the rod (see the photos in the baitcasting reel section) and the guides running out along the upper side of the rod.

The photo below shows the trigger grip that is part of the handle on bait casting rods. This allows the angler to hold the rod more firmly and still place a finger on the spool for better line control.

My Own Experience: Fifteen years ago, I used a baitcaster for the first time when fishing with Mike Parker, a friend in Texas. I struggled with backlashes all day and did not enjoy using that equipment. A few years later, I bought an expensive good-quality baitcaster, in part because the "experts" said they were better than spinning reels and I wanted to give it another shot. I used it for a few months, during which time I never learned to cast consistently without frequent backlashes. I also had some difficulty turning the relatively small handles with my large hands. Rather than spending a lot of extra time learning to cast a baitcasting reel successfully, I chose to sell the rod and reel. A few years after that, I decided to give baitcasters yet another try and again bought a good-quality baitcasting rod and reel. My experience with that combo mirrored my earlier experiences, so I sold the nearly new rod and reel.

At this point, I find that I have very good casting control with my spinning tackle and have little incentive to buy baitcasting gear in the future. Although baitcasting gear is preferred by others and fits into their fishing comfort zone, it is outside of my comfort zone.

Trolling Rods and Reels

In this section I describe the heavy rods and reels commonly used for trolling large and heavy lures. The reels are not used often for casting – instead they serve as heavy-duty winches and drag systems for winding in line, lure, and fish. In design they are larger versions of baitcasting tackle.

The large spool is oriented perpendicular to the rod. Some trolling reels offer a level-wind mechanism. On other models, the angler needs to use his/her thumb to distribute line across the width of the spool.

The larger size of trolling reels allows them to hold much greater lengths of line, which is particularly important when targeting fast and heavy big game species. When fishing in inshore settings or in the Chesapeake Bay, most anglers troll with medium sized reels and short stout rods as seen in the photo below.

When fishing offshore for larger and stronger tackle, even heavier tackle is used. The reel shown below weighs nearly 7 pounds and can hold 2,900 yards of 130-pound braided line.

Instead of a star drag system, most of the large offshore reels use a lever drag system. Some of the large offshore reels have a two-speed winding system, by which the gear ratio can be changed with a lever to optimize either speed or power.

Large reels like this are paired with very strong rods. Some offshore rods use roller guides instead of the standard ring-style guides.

My Own Experience: In my early years of fishing in the Chesapeake Bay, I bought several medium-weight trolling combos. I had little success at trolling in that way and eventually stopped doing it. The same rods I had used for trolling could be used for deep-drop bottom fishing trips. I made several trips offshore of North Carolina where the charter boat would anchor over a wreck and each angler would drop bait and sinker to the bottom (often in more than 100 feet depth). I realized that this style of fishing was not in my comfort zone. At that point I had no further use for medium or heavy trolling tackle. I sold the combos I owned.

When I fished offshore for big game on charter boats or on private boats owned by friends, I always used the rods and reels they had on board. I never owned heavy offshore gear myself.

Fly Fishing Rods and Reels

Fly rods tend to be long, thin, and flexible. Unlike spinning and baitcasting tackle, which rely on the weight of lure to pull the line from the spool during casting, the weight of the unfurling fly line in the air propels the fly to its destination. When a fish is hooked, the bending rod provides the primary resistance to fight the fish.

Rods are designed in weight classes, such as a 5-weight or a 9-weight rod. The weight rating refers to the weight of the line the rod is designed to cast. Rods with higher weight numbers are rated to cast larger diameter fly lines (sometimes measured in grains on fly line packaging) and offer greater strength for making longer casts into the wind and fighting heavier fish.

Fly lines have become quite specialized in recent years. While floating lines will suffice for most shallow water applications, fly fishers now have an array of sinking and intermediate line choices which give them access to fish in deeper waters.

Fly rods are usually built with several sections to make transporting the rod easier. Most fly rods are built from graphite or fiberglass. In addition to their weight rating, they come in different tip actions – fast, medium and slow, just like conventional rods. The can also range in length from 6 to 7 feet for small stream rods to 9 to 10 feet for applications in bigger water. In the early days of fly fishing, many rods were made from bamboo. Some fly anglers enjoy using old-fashioned bamboo rods for nostalgic reasons. Fly rods have reel seats and guides like the other types of rods.

Most of the time fly reels serve as line storage devices. Unlike spinning and baitcasting reels, which move lures by turning the reel handle, flies are moved by "stripping" or pulling line back toward you by hand. If you hook a small fish, you can often bring the fish in fully by hand, without using the reel. However, if you hook a stronger fish, you can use the reel and its drag system to offer greater resistance to the fish and to wind it in. You can also "palm" the edges of the reel with your hand as the reel revolves with outgoing line to slow a fast-moving strong fish.

The photo below shows a fly reel with a small handle in the upper left section. The fly line is considerably thicker than line used on spinning or baitcasting reels. Note that the reel sits almost at the end of the rod, making most of the rod available for bending.

Photo Credit: Mark Bange

Reels should be matched in size and strength to the fly rods on which they are used. This is critical for the balance and "feel" of the overall outfit. A well balanced rod and reel will cast more easily because the fly fisher will not need to contend with an excessively heavy (or too light) reel as a counterweight to the rod in the casting process. Larger reels hold more line. This may be needed when targeting larger and stronger fish.

My Own Experience: I only tried fly rods on two occasions when I was able to use friends' equipment for a few minutes. I did not develop any skill in casting during those short periods. I have never owned fly fishing equipment. Fly fishing offers great challenge and pleasure to many anglers, but it is outside of my fishing comfort zone.

My Own Preference in Rods and Reels

All the rods and reels I own at this time are spinning tackle. I have 12 spinning rods ranging in length from 6' to 7'.

- 2 medium heavy (one Steve Fogle Backyard Custom rod, one Carrot Stix)
- 4 medium (St. Croix – one is a travel rod)

- 2 medium light (St. Croix)
- 2 light (St. Croix)
- 2 ultralight (one Eagle Claw, one Fenwick).

All of these rods are well-made and perform nicely on the fish I target. They hold up easily in the brackish water environment in which I usually fish with just a quick rinse at the end of each trip. The rods then are stored vertically in the garage rod rack until their next use. In the past, I have owned longer rods, but found they did not meet my needs or were hard to use in my kayaks. Eventually I sold them and replaced them with rods of 6' or 6'6". I do have two 7' rods today. They work fine but are at the edge of my preference range. When fishing from a kayak, I find the extra length makes it more difficult to gain control of a fish or to untangle a tip wrap. When casting from the Scout or my kayaks, the extra length presents more opportunities to bang into something on a back cast.

I use my rods often and find that periodically I will break off the tip of a rod. If the broken section is large, the rod must be retired or returned to the manufacturer if under warranty. But when the broken tip section is only a few inches long, I generally replace the tip guide with a new one. You can do this yourself if you have the part or can have it done at a tackle shop or by a rod repair shop. Several of the rods listed above are a few inches shorter today than when they were new. The power of the rod is changed slightly, but the rods still perform well.

All the rods are paired with the same model of spinning reel – Shimano Stradic -- in sizes including 1000, 2500, and 3000. I have several brand new Stradic reels in my garage tackle inventory to replace the existing Stradics when they wear out. These reels hold up well in brackish and salt water. Like the rods, they get a quick shot with a hose after each trip.

With only that relatively modest arsenal of rods and reels, I manage to catch hundreds of striped bass, white perch, pickerel, and smaller numbers of many other species each year. During the past year, those rods and reels caught a 34" striped bass, a 36" bluefish, a 36" sand bar shark, and a 38" redfish, along with many other fish of myriad species.

Each of these combos can be used in multiple ways to catch fish. For example, I have caught fish on the same medium rod by casting, jigging, and trolling light lures – all on the same trip. By choosing high quality equipment that serves more than one function, I am able to keep my tackle inventory streamlined and manageable for storage.

In my earlier fishing years, I often bought less expensive rods and reels, thinking I was getting a bargain. I remember trying two different brands of reels recently imported from Asia. They featured a high number of bearings and were touted by the tackle shop owner as a great deal for the money. The reels performed well for half a season. By mid-summer, several of the metal components showed substantial corrosion as a result of the manufacturer using lower quality metal alloys. After the first year, those reels looked worn and were rough and noisy to use. Although the purchase price was low, the cost per year was high as I needed to dispose of the reels after a year or two.

Over time, I realized how much I enjoyed fishing and how using higher quality equipment would make my fishing experience easier and less tiring. I gradually upgraded to higher quality rods and reels.

I'm sure my wife cannot understand why anyone would need 12 fishing rods. Yet compared to most recreational anglers and especially those who fish more than 100 days a year as I do, 12 rods is a modest collection. By moving away from the fishing styles I did not enjoy practicing, I was able to reduce the amount of gear I needed. By focusing on spinning tackle of similar brands and models, I am comfortable with the performance I get from my gear and can switch back and forth seamlessly.

I know that some anglers love to have numerous rods and reels that are optimized for a particular style of fishing. They believe that having one dedicated rod for LTJ and another dedicated rod for topwater and another for casting to breaking fish helps them catch more fish. They may be right and certainly are within their fishing comfort zone. However, I don't feel that I am missing out on many fish because I don't use separate rods for every fishing niche.

<u>Rigging My Spinning Rods</u>

Main Lines: When I started out fishing, nearly all line was monofilament (mono). In the past few decades, new technologies were introduced. One important innovation is braided line using tightly wound Spectra fiber that has much lower diameter than mono line of the same strength. Braided line offers very little stretch. This increases the sensitivity, allowing anglers to feel the slightest tap on their lures.

At this point I run braid on all my rods. I started using Powerpro brand braided line years ago, and stuck with that brand. Other brands are fine too. I prefer using bright yellow so I can see the line. I always add a mono or fluorocarbon leader to reduce the visibility of the line next to the lure and to aid in lifting the fish from the water. I have heard from others that mono is a good choice when throwing topwater lures. Since I rarely throw topwater (hard plastic plugs), there is no incentive for me to spool up that way.

There are several different philosophies about how to spool your reel with braid. You should not place braid directly onto a bare spool (I did that years ago and watched the entire bundle of line spin around the metal spool when I had resistance on the line). Many people make several wraps to half a spool of inexpensive mono line on the spool as backing then tie braid on for the rest of the spool. This reduces costs – braid is more expensive than mono. But it introduces an extra knot into the line bundle. This knot can catch during a cast and cause the cast to fall short.

I use a different approach. It consumes more braid, but in the scheme of things, an extra few dollars of braid (which does not need to be changed out every year like mono) is a minor incremental cost. I start by wrapping masking tape or some other tape around the bare spool. Last summer I was away from home without any masking tape and needed to respool a reel. I took two band aids from my travel kit, trimmed the width to match the spool, and used them to cover the spool. The tape backing allows the braid to dig in and not slip on the spool. I usually place the feed spool of braid in a bucket, bring the end of the line through the rod guides, and tie a knot around the spool. I grip the line between the reel and first guide to apply some tension and begin winding. Then I fill the spool about 80-90% with braid. Don't fill it all the way to the flange on the edge of the spool. This amount of line serves me for several years. I do occasionally get a wind knot or a snag and have to cut off a few feet. Eventually the remaining length on the spool is not enough for a long cast – then I respool.

I use 10-lb braid on my 1000 series reels and 20-lb braid on all the other reels. Unless you are targeting huge fish, this is plenty of line strength.

The downside of using braid is that it does not stretch. If you hook a lure over one the rod guides and tighten the line, you have potential to pop out a ceramic ring. Also if you reel a fish in with only a foot or so of line out, and the fish lunges, you can break off a rod tip. The other hazard of thin braided line is that it can easily cut your skin. If you snag a lure, do not grab the line and tug hard – you are likely to get cut. I have personal experience with all of these mishaps.

Leaders: For fishing here in the Chesapeake Bay with relatively low water clarity, I use 20-pound mono leaders on my reels spooled with 10-pound braid and 25-pound mono or fluorocarbon leaders on the reels spooled with 20-pound braid. I keep things consistent, making it easy to remember which reel gets a particular line/leader combination. When fishing in locations with clear water, I use fluorocarbon leaders.

I do not use long leaders – typically 12" to 24". Each time I break off a lure or retie, the leader shortens. I let it get down to about 12", then cut off the leader and add a fresh one.

Leaders serve several functions. First, unless the water is highly turbid, fish can see a colored main line (I use yellow), which might discourage them from biting. The leader has lower visibility in the water. In particular, fluorocarbon leader has an optical density very close to that of water and may come close to disappearing in the water. Second, the leader offers greater resistance to abrasion than the braid and may help to catch more fish that would have broken off.

Third, when I catch a fish on a braided line and get the fish next to the boat, I try to grab the line close to the lure to control the fish. If I grab the braid, and the fish lunges, I can easily get a cut in my finger. By adding a mono or fluorocarbon leader, I have a thicker line to grab. As I write this chapter, I look down at the index finger on my left hand and see a partially healed line cut from a productive striped bass trip I made last week. For part of the trip I used a leader that was too short and ended up grabbing the braided main line several times to lift heavy fish. My finger paid the price.

If you catch a strong fish or think the line has rubbed up against something sharp, like oyster shells or barnacles, you should run your fingers along the leader to check for nicks. If you find a nick or heavily abraded section, cut off that section or add a new leader.

Knots: There are many different knots used by fishermen. Like the other components of my tackle system, I try to keep things simple by consistently using the same few knots. When I first learned each knot, I practiced them at home in the garage repeatedly until I could tie them easily. It is much tougher to tie a knot when in a kayak in cold weather than in my garage at home. The practice pays off.

Here are the knots I use. Rather than making extensive drawings showing how these knots are tied, I refer readers to various internet sites that show static images and even videos for tying many types of knots.

Leader-to-Lure - I use two types of knots for tying a leader to a lure depending on the circumstances. For most of my lures (e.g., jigheads, bucktails, metal jigs and spoons) I use a loop knot. This creates a small loop that allows the lure to swing or swim as it is pulled along. I began using this knot in 2014 after observing several successful fishing guides using it – my catch rate went up noticeably that year and has stayed up.

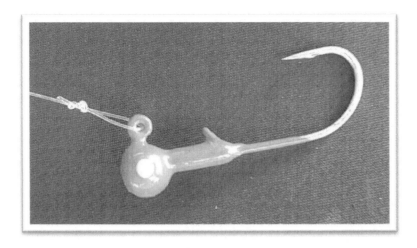

On some lures (e.g., a small spinnerbait with an open bend for tying onto the line, a lure that already has a split ring, or a snap swivel), a loop knot would not work. Here I use the Palomar knot, which snugs down tightly and holds well.

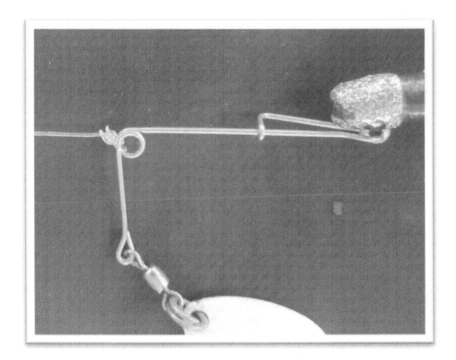

<u>Main Line to Leader</u> - I use the double uni knot. There are other popular knots for this purpose. I checked them out and found them more difficult to tie. I stick with the double uni knot. I typically make four wraps on each individual uni knot before tightening the knot. If you are worried about the knot slipping, add a few more wraps on each uni knot. The photo shows a double uni knot connecting 10-pound braid and 20-pound mono line. The resulting knot is slender enough to pass through the rod tip and other guides.

<u>Loop on the Main Line</u> - If I want to add a second lure above the primary lure, I can pinch together a section of line and tie a surgeon's loop knot (sometimes called a double surgeon's loop). I can use the resulting loop directly or can snip off one end of the loop to make a longer single leg. This necessarily affects the main line. To remove the knot it is necessary to cut off the main line above the loop.

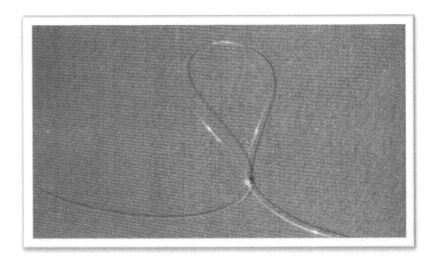

Over the past two years I have tried a different method of attaching a second lure. I take a 15" piece of 20-pound or heavier mono, attach one end to the lure and tie a surgeon's loop knot on the other end.

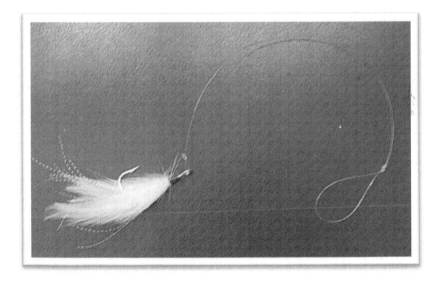

I place the new line under the main line above the line/leader knot. I pass the lure through the loop on the other end and pull it tight. The lure is connected to the main line above the knot and can slide up and down during the fight if necessary. If you want to remove this, you can snip off the attached section of line without damaging the main line. I have used this approach for light tackle trolling with a tandem rig and for LTJ.

On a recent striper jigging trip, I fished a 2-oz Stingsilver metal lure on the end of the line and a large fly attached above the line/leader knot as described above. I hooked large fish on both lures and struggled to make headway winding them in. After a few minutes, I felt a "pop" – this was the fly breaking loose from the top piece of line. I landed the fish on the bottom (a fat 31" striper) but have no idea how large the lost fish was.

Chapter 5 – Lure Types and My Comfort Zone

In this chapter I talk about different types of lures. There are thousands of different lures on the market in many colors, shapes, and sizes. I talk about several basic types of lures. I personally use just a few lure types frequently (soft plastics on jigheads or bucktails, small spinnerbaits, and large metal jigging lures) – this is my comfort zone and helps me keep my tackle inventory and storage under control. For the other lure types that I do not use often or at all, I provide a quick review.

Because I do not fly fish or fish offshore any longer, I chose not to discuss bay or offshore trolling lures or flies at all in this chapter.

On nearly all of my lures I crimp the barbed part of the hook with a pair of pliers. I keep very few fish that I catch. The barbless hook allows for a quicker release and less damage to the fish's mouth. In the infrequent event that I get jabbed with a hook, the lack of a barb makes it easier to remove the hook from my flesh.

As noted in the previous chapter for rods and reels, my lure selection overlaps somewhat with the lures used by other local fishing authors. Each of us has our own preferred styles and brands of lures. Readers are encouraged to check out those books to gain additional insight on lure selection and why those lures are preferred by each author.

Lead Heads

Jigheads: Jigheads are lures used with different types of soft plastics. They consist of a lead head and a hook embedded in the lead. The lead provides weight to cast the soft plastic and to sink it to the desired depth. The soft plastic tail is threaded onto the hook and pushed up against the lead head.

Jigheads come in a wide range of sizes. I have used 1/16-ounce size for panfish and very heavy jigheads to jig for halibut in deep water in Alaska. The photo shows two 24-ounce jigheads (one with large twister tail) along with 3/8-ounce and 1-ounce size jigheads. Most of the jigheads I use range from 1/8 ounce to 1.5 ounces.

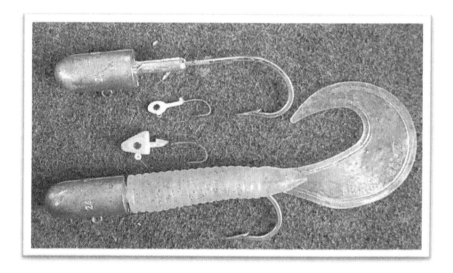

The lead heads can be molded in many different shapes. Examples of different styles can be seen in the photos included in the following sections.

Bucktails: Another version of jighead includes hair (usually from the tail of a deer) or artificial fibers that are tied just below the lead head. These lures are known as bucktails. The bundle of hair pulsates as it moves through the water. Bucktails can be used by themselves or with soft plastic tails. The first photo below shows two small bucktails with a little bit of flash tied in with the hair. The second photo shows 3" paddletails on a plain jighead and two bucktails.

Photo Credit: Mark Bange

Nearly all jigheads are made with J-hooks. Last year I bought some jigheads made with circle hooks. I prefer using circle hooks when bottom fishing, and wanted to see how they worked on jigheads. The photo below shows two jigheads with J-hooks and the bottom one with a circle hook.

I caught some fish trolling and casting with the circle hook jighead, but did not feel they performed as well as the standard J-hook jigheads. I had some bites that never hooked up solidly. I did not notice a significant difference in deep hooking – I experienced a very low deep-hooking rate with either style of jighead. In fact, since I did not crimp the barb on the circle hook, I had more difficulty removing the circle hook from some fish's mouths than I did with the barbless J-hook.

Shad Darts: Another variety of very small lead head is the shad dart. These lightweight lures have angled lead heads that usually are painted in bright colors and trimmed with some hair. They are often fished on tandem rigs with two shad darts or a shad dart and tiny spoon. When shad are migrating in the spring, the shad darts are cast into the current and may be slammed by active shad. The photo shows two shad caught on the same tandem rig with two shad darts.

Soft Plastic Lures

Soft plastic lures are available in hundreds of shapes, sizes, and colors. Most of the basic shapes are made to look like things that fish would choose to eat. For example, worms, minnows, lizards, frogs, and crawfish are common patterns. Other shapes do not look much like real prey items to me, but as they move through the water, they attract interest from the fish.

Some lures are designed to swim or wiggle naturally as they are pulled through the water. Twister tails and paddletails are great examples of these. Other shapes do not have a natural swimming motion. They must be twitched, hopped, or retrieved in a particular way in order to make them look like they are prey items.

I begin this review of soft plastic lures with the three types I use most often – twister tails, paddletails, and jerkbaits. I rarely use other styles of soft plastics.

Twister Tails: The first soft plastic lure I ever used was a 3" twister tail on a small jighead. That combination worked well when casting to breaking stripers near Thomas Point Light more than twenty years ago. Twister tails (sometimes called grubs) have a thick, usually ribbed section attached to a flexible floppy tail. The tail pulsates as it is moved through the water and simulates a swimming baitfish.

Most of the time, I stick with 3" to 4" twister tails on jigheads of ¼-ounce to ½-ounce size.

I use twister tails for surface casting into breaking fish and casting over hard bottom areas and bouncing the lure back to the boat. In addition to casting, twister tails can be trolled or jigged.

I also use Berkley Gulp twister tails throughout the year. They are made from a firmer type of plastic compound that absorbs and holds scent. Gulp baits are stored in a scented fluid. Fish may be attracted by the scent and may hold on longer after the initial bite because the taste is more realistic than regular soft plastic. I prefer those styles of Gulp that have a strong wiggle in the tail, such as the 3" and 4" swimming mullet and the 2" minnow grub. Some days they outperform standard soft plastic tails, but on other days, the standard tails produce more fish.

Paddletails: My favorite style of soft plastic lure these days is a paddletail. These are designed to mimic the profile of a baitfish with a tail structure that wiggles as the lure is moved through the water. Depending on the time of year and which species I am targeting, I fish with 3" to 5" paddletails and different weights of jigheads or bucktails. The shape and flexibility of the plastic gives different swimming motions to the paddletails. My favorite paddletails are 3" Fat Sam mullets made by 12 Fathom lure company. They have an excellent swimming motion at low, medium, and high speed. Other brands of paddletails work well too, but I prefer the Fat Sam.

The photo shows a variety of types and sizes of paddletails attached to jigheads ranging from 1/8 ounce (bottom right) to 1.5 ounce (middle left). The Fat Sam mullets are on the bottom and the second from the top on the right column. Two of the lures are attached to bucktails. When fished on bucktails, I prefer using longer paddletails with slender tails that stick out past the hair on the bucktails. The third and fourth lures in the right column are twister tails.

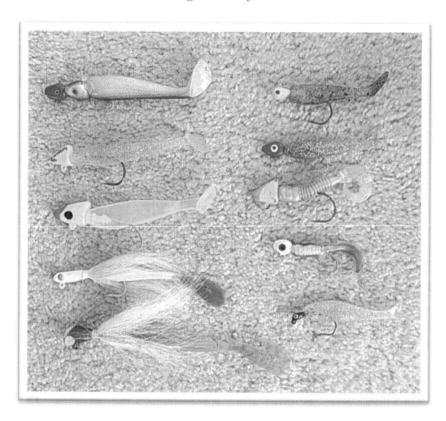

Bluefish have sharp teeth. When they are around, they make quick work of most twister tails and paddletails. If I get too many bite offs, I switch to lures made with a stretchier plastic compound (e.g., Z-Man plastics). These are resistant to many bluefish bites and allow the angler to keep fishing without changing out lures frequently. I have some difficulty keeping the stretchier plastic tails in place on the jighead. I use them only when bluefish are around and switch back to standard soft plastics at other times.

Other options when bluefish are around are to switch to metal spoons or to break out my "expendable plastics" box. Most of us have soft plastic lures around the house that we do not like for some reason and don't plan to use. Rather than throwing them away, I place them in a separate tackle tray. When I get into aggressively feeding bluefish, I pick plastics from the expendable box and let the bluefish have their way. The first photo shows the expendable box, and the second photo shows the results of many aggressive bluefish – note the absence of any floppy tails.

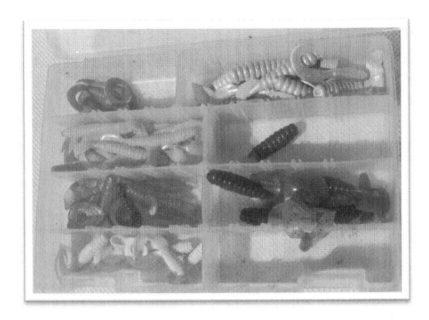

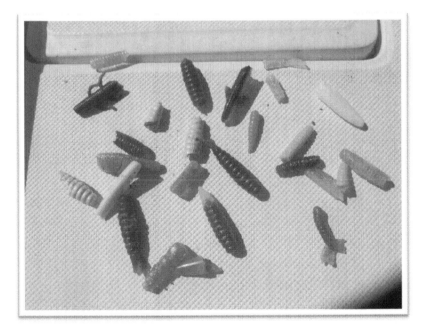

Larger paddletails are often used with heavy trolling tackle on umbrella rigs, parachutes, or bucktails. They are referred to as shads and can be 9" or longer.

Another style of paddletail embeds the lead head inside the plastic to make a one-piece lure. These swim shads can be found in different sizes, shapes, and colors as seen in the photo. Over the past few years, I caught large stripers and bluefish on these lures. I once caught a large carp by trolling the lure on the bottom left. One downside to swim shads is that once the plastic is damaged, the lure is no longer usable – you cannot readily reuse the lead head inside the body.

I have also fished with soft plastic shrimp that have hooks imbedded inside. I have not had much success with plastic shrimp in the mid-Chesapeake region as those large shrimp are not a typical local prey item for the fish. They work better in Florida, where live shrimp are a common bait type.

Jerkbaits: The term "jerkbait" can be used for both soft plastic and hard plastic lures. In this section, just the soft plastic types are discussed. Soft plastic jerkbaits are long slender baits that have a narrow tail. When retrieved slowly they offer little active swimming motion. But by adding appropriate movement while retrieving, they show a much more seductive swimming motion that attracts fish. If they are retrieved rapidly with a bit of twitching, they look like a fleeing baitfish.

Another common use for soft plastic jerkbaits is jigging. The LTJ technique relies heavily on larger jerkbaits. The photo below shows several styles of jerkbaits with and without jigheads.

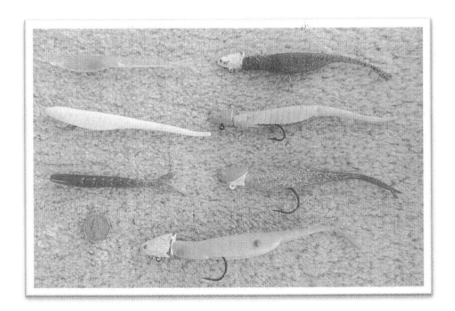

The next photo shows some 10" BKDs (Bass Kandy Delights), the type of soft plastic jerkbait I have used most often (I also use the 6" size).

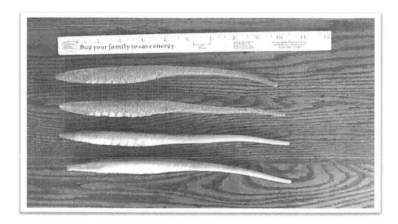

In January 2016 I had an outstanding day catching numerous stripers to 34" while jigging 10" BKDs and other large jerkbaits in the lower Chesapeake Bay.

Other Styles of Soft Plastics: I rarely use soft plastic lures other than the three types described above – they are outside my fishing comfort zone. Many anglers, particularly bass fisherman, carry dozens of styles of soft plastics with them and change out styles and colors frequently. Given my unfamiliarity with those lures, I discuss them together in this section.

Plastic worms are traditional soft plastic baits for bass. They are sold in numerous colors and sizes. Some have a tapered tail while others have a twister tail.

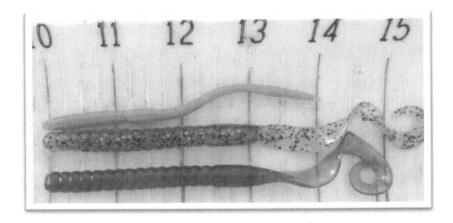

The style of worm shown below is called "Senko". While less flexible than most plastic worms, they are effective at catching bass.

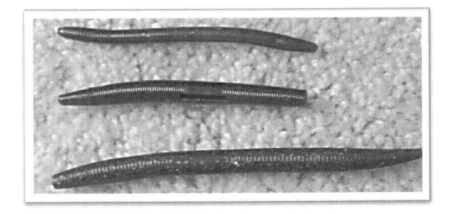

Worms, like the other types of plastics reviewed in this section, can be rigged in various ways. However since I rarely fish freshwater, rigging methods for worms and other lures in this section are not discussed. Readers who wish to learn more about rigging these plastics are advised to seek information online or in other books about "Texas Rigs" and "Carolina Rigs". Both methods employ special hooks with bent shafts that firmly grip the plastic baits and the use of slip sinkers to reach the depths where fish are holding.

Another common style of soft plastic lure is the tube bait. This lure has numerous floppy tentacles that wave about as the lure is jigged up and down.

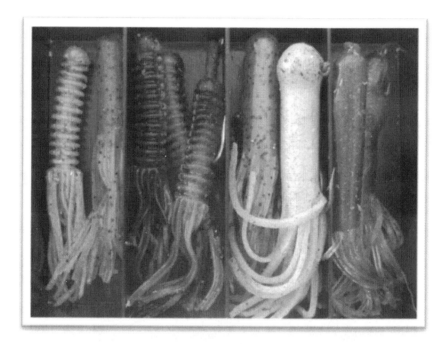

Other plastic lures are shaped like animals that could be found in the environments where the bass live. Examples include frogs, crawfish, lizards, and so-called creature baits.

Spinners

Another common class of lures adds one or more spinner blades to a lure to give additional vibration and flash as the lure is retrieved. I split spinners into two groups depending on whether the blade is attached directly to the lure shaft (inline spinners) or is offset on an angled piece of wire (spinnerbaits). Examples of both are shown in the following paragraphs.

Inline Spinners: Inline spinners consist of one or more blades, a sliding weight, and a hook, all attached to the same shaft. As inline spinners move through the water, the blade(s) swing around. Most inline spinners are made with treble hooks. As noted in an earlier chapter, I do not like using treble hooks. Today I rarely use inline spinners, but when I did use them, I often clipped off one or two of the hooks on the treble (for example, see the smallest spinner in the next photo).

The inline spinners I have used are generally small, although larger sizes are available for large prey such as the Musky Killer lure on the right in the photo.

Spinnerbaits: Spinnerbaits can be found in most freshwater bass anglers' tackle boxes. Spinnerbaits are made with a bent wire that puts one or more blades at an angle offset from the part of the wire holding the hook and a lead head. Large spinnerbaits come with a variety of sizes and shapes of blades. Many of the jigheads are adorned with floppy plastic skirts.

Most spinnerbaits are fished without a soft plastic tail on the hook. I do not often throw large spinnerbaits, but have used the Redfish Magic lure shown below with a 3" paddletail to catch largemouth bass, blue catfish, and redfish.

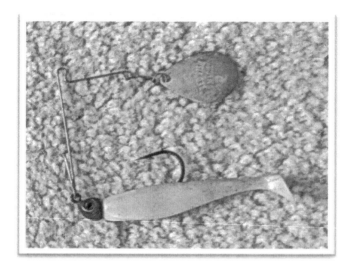

Spinnerbaits are available with an open or closed bend in the wire. Most of the lures shown in the previous two photos have open bends. A snug-fitting knot, like the Palomar knot, must be used to attach them to the line or leader. Some spinnerbaits, especially in smaller sizes, have the wire twisted to make a closed loop or rolled into a split ring. The next photo shows two small spinnerbaits. The one on the left has an open bend, while the one on the right has a closed bend. Sometimes I connect the ones with closed bends to the main line using a snap swivel.

This style of lure is my first choice for targeting white perch throughout the summer months. It also catches stripers, pickerel, and bluefish. I use various versions of these small (1/8-oz) spinnerbaits. Some use feathers, while others use artificial fibers or bucktail material. These are typically fished without soft plastic tails – the feathers, fibers, and hair bundles pulsate as they move through the water.

The lures shown in the next two photos use what I call a "spinner arm" (often called a beetle spin). The wire and blade are attached to a separate small jighead that is often adorned with a small twister tail or paddletail (next photo) or tiny bucktail (second photo). This type of lure is effective for white perch.

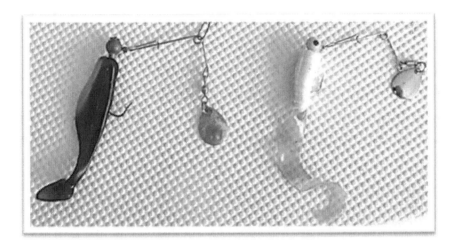

Photo credit: Mark Bange

Chatterbaits and Buzzbaits: These lures are spinnerbait variations that employ spinning or vibrating metal plates rather than blades. The first photo below shows a buzzbait. The metal plate rotates around the wire axis. The second photo shows a chatterbait with a soft plastic tail rather than a skirt. The metal plate does not rotate but vibrates up and down.

Photo Credit: Bruce Kellman

Hard Baits

One of the most common styles of lures for freshwater fishing is a hard plastic or wooden lure shaped like a small fish or other aquatic prey item like a crawfish. There are many varieties of hard baits designed for use at different depths in the water column. Some float and swim at the surface. Others are designed to dive to different depths. Other popper-type lures have a concave front end that splashes water as it is twitched across the water surface.

Many anglers are highly successful using hard baits – some consider them to be "go-to lures". Alan Battista's book on light tackle trolling from kayaks discusses how he uses diving hard baits to target large stripers suspended at deeper depths. He has great success with those lures, but I do not choose to use them very often myself – they are outside my fishing comfort zone.

Why don't I like to use hard baits? The main reason is that nearly all hard baits are rigged with two or three treble hooks. As noted previously, I do not like to use treble hooks. I have had a few occasions when I caught stripers on poppers. In nearly every case, the fish got stuck with more than one treble hook in its mouth and surrounding areas. This was hard on the fish and made quick release difficult. I rarely keep fish that I catch – I prefer to release the fish with as little trauma as possible. I have had several friends who got a treble hook stuck in their hand or leg while another treble was still in the fish's mouth. This experience was painful for the angler and was probably rough on the fish too.

I have clipped off one or two of the hooks on a treble or replaced a treble hook with a J-hook to minimize the treble hook impact. In part because of my lack of experience and confidence in these lures, I don't throw them often. When I do throw them, I do not catch many fish with them. This negative feedback reinforces my decision not to use them. Although I have owned many hard baits in the past, I own only 5 hard baits at this time. The rest of this section gives a brief overview and shows some examples.

Crankbaits: Crankbaits are lures that are retrieved or trolled at speeds that cause the lures to dive to different depths. They are built with plastic or metal bills in the front that cause the lure to dive to different depths depending on bill size and shape and speed through the water. Most crankbaits wobble somewhat as they are moved through the water. The resulting vibrations help to attract fish. Some offer exaggerated wobbling – these are often called jerkbaits (different from the soft plastic jerkbaits previously described). Some models of lures are hollow with a ball bearing inside that rattles as the lure is moved.

The next photo shows three long slender crankbaits with different length bills. The bottom lure is jointed to give it a more realistic swimming motion.

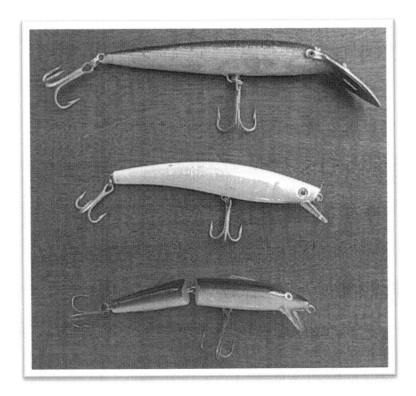

The next photo shows a variety of shorter and fatter crankbaits. Some have bills – some do not.

Topwater Plugs: Many anglers claim that fishing topwater lures is their favorite way to catch fish. That is great for them, but topwater has not been an effective technique for me. I will leave this technique and style of lure to others who have better success. It remains outside my fishing comfort zone most of the time.

Topwater plugs typically float. Swimming topwater plugs are cast out, and moved in short twitches. A popular technique for fishing topwater lures is known as "walking the dog". On the first rod twitch, the lure moves a short way to the left. On the next twitch of the rod, the lure turns and moves a short way to the right. The lure moves slowly back and forth during the retrieve.

The next photo shows a popular brand of swimming topwater plug.

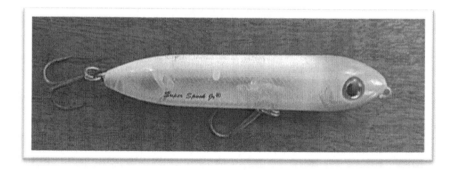

Here is the same lure, effectively inhaled by a small striper. Several prongs of the front treble hook are stuck in the fish's mouth. After catching that fish, I removed the lure and replaced it with a jighead and plastic.

Another category of topwater lure is the popper. The lures have a concave-shaped face that splashes and throws off water as the lure is "popped" across the surface. The popping and splashing can attract fish to smash the lure, sometimes missing the hooks and tossing the lure into the air.

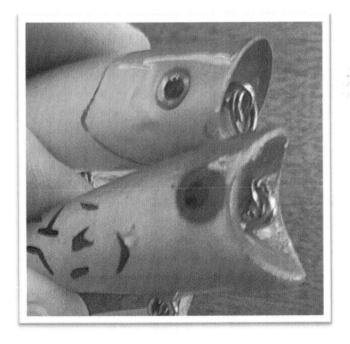

These same lures are shown below in full profile. The larger popper has been modified by removing the front treble and replacing the rear treble with a J-hook with hair.

Metal Spoons

Metal spoons are simple and effective lures. They range from thin, curved, lightweight metal lures to heavier solid metal lures that can be jigged or retrieved. A few examples are given below.

Thin Swimming Spoons: I rarely use this style of lure, but know other anglers who love using them. They are meant to be cast and retrieved or trolled. The curved shape of the lure makes them wobble as they move through the water. Some are sold with trebles, other with J-hooks. The Mepps spoon in the bottom photo had the original treble replaced by a single hook with hair.

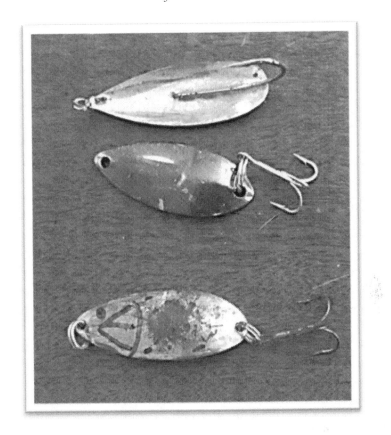

On the lower end of the size scale is a tiny silver or gold spoon used for shad fishing. These are roughly 1" long.

Compact Solid Metal Lures: This group of lures ranges from about 1 ounce to more than 3 ounces in weight. They generally have a long slender profile. Given that shape and their weight, these lures can be cast a long way. The larger ones sink rapidly when used for jigging. If the lures come with treble hooks, I replace them with standard hooks.

The next two photos show some of the smaller (less than 1 ounce) and medium (1 to 2 ounces) sized lures in this group. They can be cast and retrieved, bounced along the bottom, or trolled.

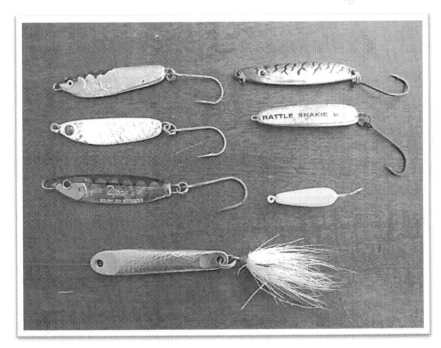

The largest lures in this group (2-4 ounces) are generally used for jigging. The top lure in the next photo is made using a 2-ounce trolling sinker (drail) and a large fly for the hook.

Anglers jigging in deep marine waters may use considerably larger metal jigs.

Other Types of Lures

Some lure styles are popular in one region of the country or in another country. For example, I bought several Kiwi lures when I visited New Zealand. These are brightly colored plastic shells with wings surrounding a hollow lead core. The hook can be fastened to the plastic shell, or the main line can be threaded through the hollow core so that the lure wobbles along the main line.

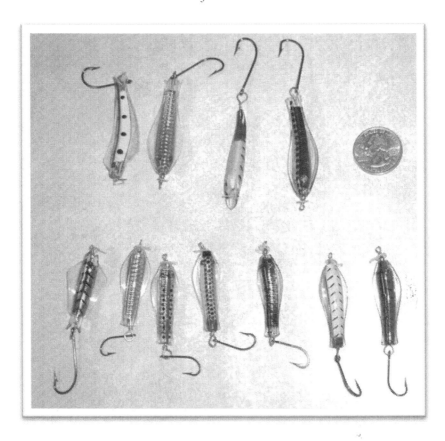

These lures are trolled in New Zealand lakes for large trout. They are effective there, but I have not had much success with them here at home. Nevertheless it was fun to buy them and try them out.

Many types of lures are used for fishing in ways that I personally do not practice. In keeping with the theme of this book – finding your fishing comfort zone, I encourage readers to seek out unique lure types that match the styles of fishing you enjoy the most.

Part Three: Fishing Methods and Rigging Tips

Chapter 6 – My Fishing Calendar

In the next few chapters I talk about the different ways that I like to fish. Nearly all of my fishing is done through casting, jigging, and light-tackle trolling. Occasionally I bottom fish using bait. There are many other ways to fish, such as heavy tackle trolling, fly fishing, livelining, and floating live bait under a bobber. Those techniques are effective in catching fish and are enjoyed by millions of anglers. But for me, they are outside my fishing comfort zone. This chapter is limited to those methods I actually use.

I also refer readers to Lenny Rudow's book "Rudow's Guide to Fishing the Chesapeake Bay" for descriptions of Chesapeake Bay fishing methods beyond what I describe in the following chapters.

<u>My Annual Fishing Cycle</u>

Before getting into the details of the specific fishing techniques, I want to explain how I choose to fish throughout the year. This cycle is not tightly fixed – it does evolve over time.

January-March: Most of my local winter fishing is done from my kayak in the tidal creeks and coves of the Severn River. Chain pickerel is the target species. I cast lures or live minnows for the pickerel.

During this time of year, some other kayak anglers troll diving crankbaits or other lures for large stripers found in deeper water. However, I personally do not fish from my kayak in deep open water during the winter.

April – May: I begin trolling 4" to 6" paddletails on light tackle in the Severn River for stripers. At some point (usually in early May) large stripers move into the river and can be found in specific locations for a few weeks. They are typically spread out enough that jigging or casting is not as productive as trolling.

A few times each spring I travel an hour north to the lower Susquehanna River to fish for migrating shad. I cast shad darts, tiny spoons, or little twister tails into the current to catch the fish moving upstream.

During early to mid-May, the white perch return to the shallow shoreline areas in the Severn River and its tidal tributaries. I fish for them from May to October by casting small spinnerbaits.

June-September: For me, these are the most enjoyable fishing months. The air and the water are warm, and I do not worry about wearing heavy clothing. I continue trolling paddletails from my kayaks in the Severn River for stripers, although the average size of the stripers drops after the three-week pulse of bigger fish in early May. I decrease the size of the paddletails from 4" or 5" to 3" to better mimic the baitfish in the area. I use the same light tackle kayak trolling techniques to fish shallow water spots near Kent Narrows and in Eastern Bay from my kayak. I cast for white perch in the Severn creeks.

I begin to use my center console for fishing in the main Chesapeake Bay and in Eastern Bay. I ride around a route of fishing spots looking for diving birds, breaking fish, or good sonar marks on the fishfinder. Depending on whether the fish are near the surface or near the bottom, I cast to them or jig with heavier lures. I cast to large structures, either permanent facilities like bridge pilings, or other temporary structure items that remain in an area long enough to attract a population of baitfish and predators. Paddletails, twister tails, and small metal lures are very effective for this style of fishing. I also spend some time jigging on the same structures (LTJ) using soft plastic jerkbaits on jigheads or 2-ounce metal lures.

I enjoy taking the center console into remote shallow areas in Eastern Bay where I can use my trolling motor to move around stump fields and shallows near sod banks and cast for stripers, perch, or an occasional redfish or speckled trout.

For the past few years, I have made a late summer road trip to the lower Eastern Shore of Virginia. The peninsula is narrow there, allowing easy access to both the ocean side and the Chesapeake Bay side. I fish with my center console in the ocean-side marshes, near the Chesapeake Bay Bridge Tunnel (CBBT), and in open bay waters. This is one of the few times during the year when I spend some time doing bottom fishing with squid, shrimp, or live minnows. There are dozens of species living there – I often catch more than ten species over a few days of bottom fishing there. I also like to cast soft plastic lures and larger spinnerbaits to catch stripers, trout, redfish, and other species.

October – December: As the air and water cool off, the Severn River fishing undergoes a transition. The white perch leave their shallow shoreline habitats, and the pickerel that inhabit the same zones are caught more frequently. Pickerel fishing is usually quite good from mid-October through mid-December. As the winter progresses into the following year, pickerel fishing remains available, but the bite slows down. If the stripers remain in the river as they did in 2015, I continue to troll for them in my kayak.

I continue fishing in the main Chesapeake Bay and in Eastern Bay in my center console until late November, when I put it away for the year.

Other Fishing: Throughout the year, I like to visit Tampa, FL for a few days at a time to kayak fish with a guide in the shallow flats and next to mangrove islands. We usually cast 1/8-oz jigheads with 3" to 4.5" soft plastic tails. We catch a lot of speckled trout, ladyfish, and flounder, and get an occasional snook or redfish.

I fish several times each year with local light tackle guide, Capt. Walleye Pete Dahlberg. Winter trips usually involve jigging large soft plastic jerkbaits at warm water power plant discharges or jigging on schools of stripers in deep water. Summer trips often involve crossing to the remote Eastern shore marshes and islands and casting for stripers and speckled trout in shallow water environments.

Nearly all my fishing is done in saltwater. I do enjoy a few kayak fishing trips to nearby freshwater ponds, and have had success catching snakeheads and largemouth bass when fishing with Capt. Mike and Capt. Dave of Indian Head Charters on tidal freshwater Mattawoman Creek off of the Potomac River. The photo shows the 29" snakehead I caught with Capt. Dave in July 2015.

My shad fishing each spring in the Susquehanna River is about the only other freshwater fishing I do.

Chapter 7 – Casting Methods

<u>My Approach to Casting</u>

Equipment: Much of the fishing I do throughout the year involves casting with spinning rods. I use ultralight or light spinning rods for casting small lures to pickerel, white perch, shad, and other smaller species. I use light, medium light, or medium spinning rods to cast slightly larger lures to stripers, bluefish, speckled trout, and other species.

All my rods are rigged using the same pattern. The spool is filled with 10- to 20-pound braid and attached to a 20-pound mono or fluorocarbon leader. The only knots are the line/leader knot (double-uni knot) and the knot to attach the lure to the leader (loop knot or Palomar knot).

Lures: Few of the lures I cast weigh more than $\frac{1}{2}$ ounce – most are lighter. I do not cast diving crankbaits or other heavy lures that drop down far into the water column. Therefore, most of the lures I use are moving in the top few feet of water. Occasionally I slow down my retrieve and can keep a $\frac{1}{2}$-ounce lure bouncing the bottom in 10 foot depth.

When casting for white perch, I used primarily 1/8-ounce spinnerbaits to shallow water shoreline spots. My favorite perch spinners are the feather spinners made by Woody Tillery (sold as either Maryland Tackle or Woody's Tackle – left in photo) and a similar style using mostly artificial hair made by local angler Stu Sklar (Bignose spinners – right in photo). Occasionally I throw a jighead with a twister tail or a Gulp paddletail.

For stripers and bluefish, I start off throwing 3" paddletails or 4" Gulp twister tails on 1/4-ounce to ½-ounce jigheads.

If you look closely at the hook point on the next photo of a Gulp twister tail, you can see a tiny fish that was impaled on the hook as I retrieved the lure. That is quite possibly the smallest fish I ever hooked.

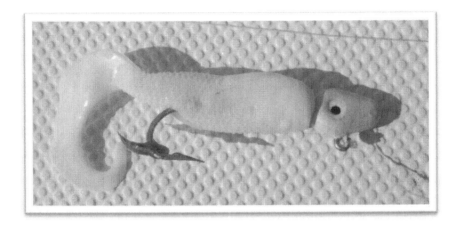

If the bite is fast, I may experiment by throwing other soft plastic tails or metal spoons. All of the lures shown in the next photo caught small bluefish and stripers during a single 3-hour trip in 2014.

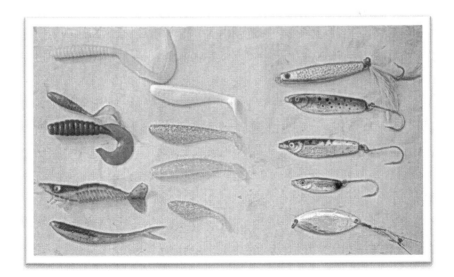

I generally prefer using lures in white, chartreuse, gold, silver, clear, tan, or similar colors. These seem to work the best in my local waters. But some days, it does not matter what color lure I use – the fish are interested in all colors.

When casting for redfish and speckled trout in the lower Eastern Shore, I use a combination of jigheads or large spinnerbaits tipped with plastic tails or Gulps.

When casting for shad in the spring, I employ a two-lure tandem rig with a swivel in the middle.

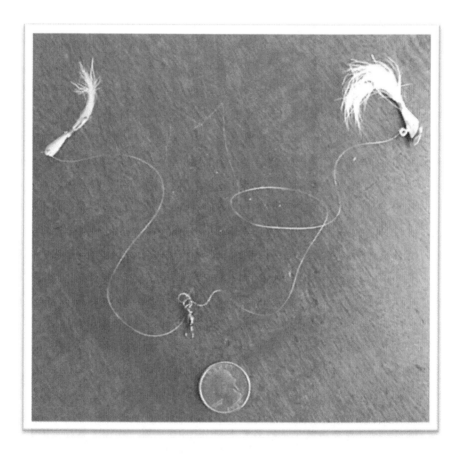

Stu Sklar showed me his version of the rig that ties separate 12" and 18" leaders to the swivel. I modified that approach somewhat by taking a 30"

piece of 20-pound mono and looping it through one end of the swivel. I adjust the lengths to give one longer end and one shorter end. I attach some combination of shad darts, small spoons, or 1/16-ounce jigheads with tiny twister tail to either end. These are cast into the moving river or stream from shore or when wading. The lures are retrieved. When the shad are running, bites are frequent.

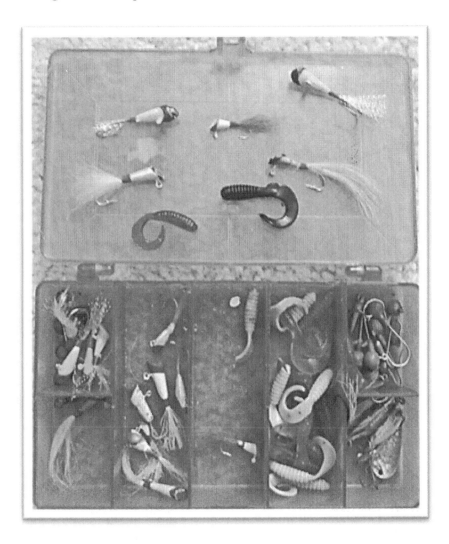

When I fish with kayak fishing guide Neil Taylor in the Tampa Bay area, we use 7' medium spinning rods with 15-pound braid and a 25-pound fluorocarbon leader (he uses fluorocarbon since the water is very clear). He generally uses 1/8-ounce Mission Fishin' jigheads with sturdy hooks to hold up to the strong game fish there. He uses three different styles of 12 Fathom brand plastic tails (Fat Sam mullet, Buzztail, and Slam-R). I catch plenty of fish on all three lures.

The photos below show a speckled trout caught on a Slam-R and a snook caught on a Fat Sam mullet.

Photo Credit: Mark Bange

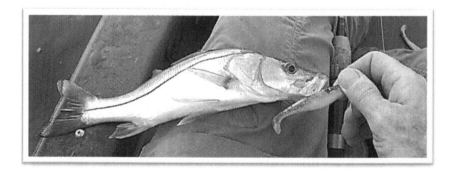

As I noted in the previous chapter, I rarely throw topwater lures, either the swimming type or poppers, or other diving hard baits. I do not have sufficient experience or expertise to offer advice on how to fish those lures.

Finding Fish: There are various pieces of information an angler can use when trying to find fish for casting:

- Breaking birds - birds actively diving on bait (look for them and/or hear them squawking)
- Birds sitting in a cluster on the water (they may be there waiting for the bait to rise to the surface again).
- Slick on the surface from chopped up baitfish (you may smell the baitfish oil before you see the slick)
- Surface swirls from feeding fish or agitated baitfish
- Bait clouds or fish arches on the fishfinder screen
- Changes in depth (lumps, holes, drop offs, edges)
- Structure
- Other fishermen in an area, particularly when they are actively catching (often called "bent-pole sonar").

Casting and Retrieving Methods: After years of fishing in small boats and kayaks, I learned to cast from a variety of angles and positions (e.g., side arm, overhead, back hand, and underhand flip). I often fished with other anglers on my small boats necessitating coordinating our back swings to avoid hooking one another. By keeping all my spinning rods used for casting within a relatively confined length range (6' to 7'), power range (ultralight to medium), and action range (fast) and using the same model of spinning reel, I have developed pretty good control and accuracy in casting.

Depending on the water depth, lure weight, and how deep I anticipate the fish are located, I may try a slow, medium, or fast retrieve. Often I use a steady retrieve (for example, when working small spinnerbaits for perch), but on some occasions, adding intermittent twitches while retrieving can stimulate a bite.

<u>Working Breaking Fish</u> - One of my favorite ways to fish is to cast into or near to breaking fish. Sophisticated retrievals are not needed here – the fish are already feeding and are likely to attack any lure in the right size range. Note that size does matter on some days. I have cast lures that looked good to me into breaking fish and had no bites. After I downsized the lures to more closely approximate the baitfish in the area, I began to get bites.

Like many anglers, I keep an eye out for working birds. When I see them actively diving on bait, there is a good chance that predatory stripers or bluefish are feeding and chasing the baitfish to the surface. On some days, I practice "run and gun" and race over to a pod of fish until they stop biting, then move on to another pod.

I recall an early fall trip to Eastern Bay in 2014. OGWLF member Scott Taylor was fishing with me. All of a sudden we heard a noise behind us that was surprisingly loud. Fish were aggressively churning up the water more than half a mile away. We quickly motored over there and began catching fish one after another.

In some cases, the breaking fish can be large, but most often they are smaller fish ranging from 12" to 16". Those fish offer great catch-and-release fishing fun when using appropriately light tackle. On occasion, there may be larger fish hanging underneath or behind the main group of breaking fish. They expend less energy than the smaller fish – they wait for chopped up baitfish to drift down to where they are located. Sometimes, I cast around the edges of the breaking fish or begin jigging to get near the bottom. My fishfinder helps in finding where the fish are located within the water column.

One hazard of casting into masses of diving birds is that it is not uncommon to snag a bird. I have never had a hook point go into a bird, but I have had quite a few cases where the braided line wrapped around a wing. When that happens, I wind the unhappy bird to my boat, cover its head with a cloth to calm it, and unwrap or snip the line. Once the bird is freed it takes off.

Bouncing on Live Bottom - I have one fishing spot near Annapolis that offers 7 to 10 foot water depth over an oyster shell bottom with deeper water nearby. I often drift over the area and cast out in all directions using ½-ounce to ¾-ounce lures with paddletails or large twister tails. I slowly bounce the lure back to the boat waiting for a bite. I have caught stripers to 27" there. The bite is not always active, but I try to make at least one drift there on each trip in that vicinity. It is not unusual to see sonar marks like the ones shown in the photo at that spot.

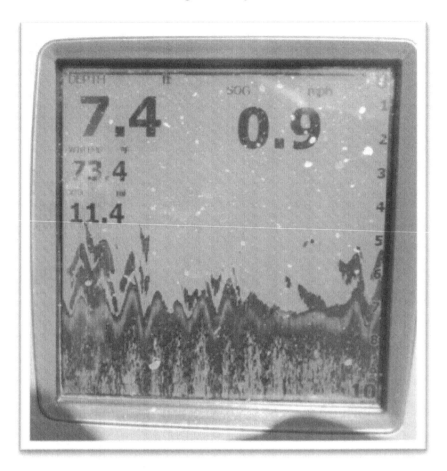

Casting to Structure - When fishing on large structure, I don't hesitate to cast in all directions to see where the fish are. Often the greatest success comes when I cast upcurrent of the structure and work the lure along the edge or side of the structure in the direction of the current flow. Natural bait is likely to be swept in that direction by the current – lures work well when they simulate natural bait behavior.

I start by casting as close to the structure as possible and initially try a medium-speed retrieve. If I don't get bites using that approach, I raise or lower the retrieval speed and may cast a bit farther away from the structure. I may count to five after the lure hits the water to allow the lure to drop a few more feet into the water before retrieving it. Sometimes the school of bait moves away from the structure, and the predators follow them. It pays to be aware of any splashing of bait or swirls near the surface to get an idea of where the fish may have moved.

On a good day, your fishfinder will light up with abundant fish marks letting you know where to cast. The next photo shows a screenshot with the entire water column filled with fish. I was able to cast to those near the surface and jig on the ones near the bottom.

Casting to Habitat Features – I enjoy casting to grass edges, sod banks, and stump fields. In most instances, I do this from my center console. I typically shut off the gas motor and drift or use the trolling motor to move stealthily around the area. My Scout offers raised platforms in the front and rear for better casting angles. I try to cast ahead or to the side of where the boat sits so I can put a lure in front of the fish before they are disturbed by the boat.

Other environments that lend themselves to this style of fishing are shallow areas near drop-offs or areas along bulkheads or rip-rap walls. When fishing next to bulkheads or rip-rap walls, look for areas that have been in place for at least several years. It takes a while for these structures to have built up enough growth to hold a small ecosystem. I have observed in the Severn River tributaries where property owners installed a new erosion protection system on their properties. Often those old natural shorelines held fish. The newer rip-rap and wooden bulkheads that replaced them are typically barren for a few years.

The water is generally shallow in these habitats. The fishfinder is not useful in showing locations of fish – rather it is used to determine whether the bottom is deep enough for further movement in the desired direction.

The photo shows fishing buddy Scott Kinnebrew on the bow of the Scout casting along a channel of a marsh on the lower Eastern Shore.

I have caught stripers to 27", redfish to 24", bluefish, speckled trout, white perch, and other species in those habitats, all while casting light lures with light and medium light spinning tackle. Here is a dandy redfish Scott caught on the same trip while casting a Redfish Magic spinnerbait to a rock wall near the CBBT.

The next photo shows Mark Bange with a gag grouper he caught while casting a paddletail to a sandy shoreline near the CBBT.

Casting for Perch and Pickerel

I devote many trips each year to casting for white perch (warmer months) and pickerel (cooler months) from my kayaks. Most of these trips are made in the Severn River, where I seek out sheltered spots in the tidal creeks and tidal ponds. Because this is such an important part of my annual fishing schedule, I am including a separate section to describe my techniques.

White Perch: White perch are absent from shallow shoreline habitats in the Severn until about mid-May. Once they show up, they can be found in many locations. I position my kayak about one cast-length from a shoreline and cast to the shore using one of my ultralight rods. Or I cast parallel to the shoreline so the lure stays in the target zone. Although I look for shorelines that offer grass beds or fallen wood, perch are so plentiful that they can be found in lots of other places too.

When I began targeting perch in the Severn more than a decade ago, I started out throwing small jigheads with white twister tails. Later I discovered spinner arms, and improved my catch rate by working the jighead and twister tail on a spinner arm. I also tried inline spinners with good success. The lure that works best for me is a 1/8-ounce spinnerbait. I typically carry two or three rods with me – each has a slightly different style of spinnerbait. I toss all of them to see which one attracts the fish best that day.

During the warm summer months, when fishing during morning or afternoon, I found that perch bite much better in shaded areas. You can work shorelines that are in the shade, or cast under docks or low bridge structures. On several days last summer, I cast using the same lures in shaded and sunny locations. I caught plenty of perch in the shade and none in the sunny spots. By evening, when the sun is low, the sun vs. shade location is less critical.

I continue targeting perch until mid-October. By then, they are moving away from shallow water toward deeper locations. They can be caught in those deeper spots using different techniques. But my preferred method is shallow water casting. Many people fish for perch with bloodworm or earthworm chunks or live grass shrimp under a bobber from early spring through fall. I don't personally fish in that way, but it is productive for filling the cooler with tasty perch.

A Very Special White Perch: I rarely find white perch in shallow Severn habitats after October. On January 1, 2012, I visited a Severn River tributary to fish for pickerel. I did catch a few pickerel that day. However, I was greatly surprised when in three feet of water depth I caught a silvery fish that was clearly not shaped like a pickerel. My initial thought was that I had caught a largemouth bass. Upon closer examination, I saw that the fish was a massive white perch! I recalled that I had caught an oversized white perch in much the same location in July 2008 and again two years later. I suspect this was the same fish that I caught three times.

I released the fish alive after some photos. The Maryland Department of Natural Resources (DNR) offers catch-and-release citations for qualifying fish. The perch was nearly 14" long, easily larger than the 13" citation-size threshold. A few weeks later I received a DNR citation.

In August of that year, I received a letter from the DNR notifying me that my citation perch qualified me for an entry in the 2012 year-long Maryland Fishing Challenge. Any person catching a citation-sized fish got an entry. I attended the awards ceremony at Sandy Point State Park in September. At the end of the awards ceremony, five names were drawn from a large drum on the stage. My name was on one of the cards. When I reached the stage, I was told to stand behind any of the five tackle bags.

P

hoto Credit: Carol Veil

The other four winners opened their bags first and had certificates for charter fishing trips. I knew there was just one prize left – a Bass Tracker boat, motor, and trailer donated by Bass Pro Shops shown in the next photo. I was truly amazed that I had won a new boat because I caught a huge white perch in a spot where it was not supposed to be in January. Of course there was a great deal of luck involved too.

Photo Credit: Carol Veil

Pickerel: For many of my early fishing years, I stopped fishing during the winter. About 2006, my local fishing club, the Severn River Rod and Keg Club, began holding a winter pickerel derby. Participants could fish from November through March as often as they liked. Qualifying fish could be entered by submitting photos of the fish next to a measuring device. I cast twister tails from the shoreline that winter and caught a surprising number of pickerel without really knowing what I was doing.

The next year, local pickerel expert Virgil Poe invited me on several pickerel trips with him in the Magothy River. He has caught thousands of pickerel from that river and has a good idea where to find them.

His advice and tutelage were invaluable in building my skill set for pickerel. I realized that I could use my kayak throughout the winter to get into sheltered creeks and ponds and sneak up on the pickerel. From then on, I fished for pickerel many times throughout the winter in the Severn River and caught hundreds of pickerel. Here are some tips on where to look for pickerel, how to rig up, and what lures or bait to use.

Where to Look for Pickerel – I do not target pickerel in the main
bay or in the main stem of the Severn River, nor do I fish in freshwater for
pickerel. I move my kayak into the sheltered tidal creeks and coves of the
Severn River. Although many sections of the shoreline look equally
attractive to my human eyes, the fish tend to locate in a few small stretches
of shoreline. After nearly a decade of fishing the same creeks and coves, I
have a pretty good idea of where to look. I look for shorelines with fallen
wood or grassy areas. I find that a wide, gradually sloping shelf is more
productive than a steeply-sloped shoreline that drops off quickly. Old docks
and bulkheads are also good choices.

Almost all the Severn pickerel I catch are in depths of 3' or less, and most
are up close to the shoreline. Sometimes you don't get a strike until the lure
is near the kayak -- in those cases, the pickerel probably followed the lure
for a while before making itself known. It pays off to paddle around the

shorelines at very low tide. You can see what the initial bottom slope is and can look for submerged structure. The following photos show examples of excellent tidal pickerel habitat. When those roots and branches are covered with water, pickerel are likely to be lurking nearby.

In most situations, don't waste time throwing your lure to open water spots of greater than 3' depth. The pickerel are rarely there. One exception is when you have very cold air temperature the night before. The surface layers of water cool down to near the air temperature, but the bottom water temperature remains in the lower 40s or upper 30s. On those mornings, I have had some luck casting to moderate-depth bowl-like areas with 3' to 6' depth.

I mentioned that perch are more likely to be in shady spots on warm, sunny days. The opposite situation can hold for pickerel on cold days. If the water body where you are fishing has shallow mud-bottomed areas on the sunny side of the water body, those areas will warm up more quickly. Baitfish are attracted to the warmth, and pickerel will follow the bait.

There are some days when the pickerel just are not biting. On those days I check out my usual stretches of shorelines and then try some places where I do not expect them to be. Usually I find no fish there either, but every now and then, I discover a new productive spot.

Rigging Up – I use 6' ultralight rods with 1000 series spinning reels. I spool with 10-pound braid and 20-pound mono leaders. I tie on 1/8-ounce jigheads.

During October, November, and early December, I fish with lures – mainly 3" paddletails or 4" Gulp twister tails. On some trips, I use the same types of small spinnerbaits I throw for perch. These work well until the water cools off. In most years, by the second week in December, the pickerel bite on lures has diminished. At that point I switch over to using live minnows that can be bought from local tackle shops.

Some anglers have good success using inline spinners or small crankbaits. I don't throw those lures for pickerel, in part because they are fitted with treble hooks that damage the pickerels' soft mouth tissue.

Using Live Minnows – To rig a live minnow on the 1/8-ounce jighead, I run the hook point from bottom to top going through the bottom lip and then out the top lip.

The minnow should be lively and wiggling. I cast it out and retrieve it just like a soft plastic lure. The speed should be slow enough to allow the pickerel to react in the cold water but fast enough to keep the minnow from contacting the bottom, where it quickly gets covered in gunk. After 10 or more casts, the minnow will no longer be lively. If I have a lot of minnows, I can remove the tired one and replace it with a lively one. This is likely to generate more bites. If I am short on minnows, I still get some bites on a listless minnow. When threading the hook through the mouth, try to make contact just behind the lips. If the hook is inserted too far back, you can hit the brain and kill the little buggers (no more wiggling).

When I buy a batch of minnows, I am likely to get a few really big ones, and lots of medium and small ones. I generally have best luck with the medium size (2" to 3" and as big around as my little finger). I buy a pint or half-pint of minnows at one time. This quantity lasts me for a few trips. I store the minnows in a minnow bucket set inside a 5-gallon bucket in my garage. Every few days, I drive to a brackish water access point, dump the old water, and add new water. Under these conditions, I can keep the minnows active for three weeks or more without any artificial aeration (note that this works in cold weather, but not in hot weather).

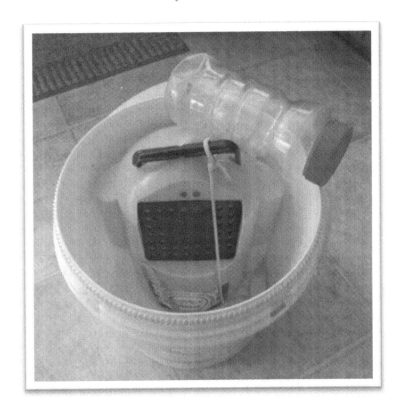

During the first few years I used minnows for pickerel fishing, I always carried the entire minnow bucket with me on the kayak. It took up a lot of space. I found an alternate method that works well for me. Before launching, I transfer several dozen minnows into a plastic dry roasted peanut jar with a screw-on lid and add water. I can leave the large minnow bucket in my van and bring along the jar.

Once underway, I transfer 5-10 minnows from the jar and place them in a cup holder or molded well in front of me. I work off of that batch until they are gone then replenish from the jar.

Catching Pickerel – The same casting approach described in the perch fishing section is used for pickerel. Cast out as close to the shoreline as possible and work the lure back at a slow speed. Try to be as quiet as possible when near your target zones. Don't drop your paddle or rod onto the kayak in a noisy way. When pedaling or paddling, use gentle quiet strokes. I have found that when I make a circuit of a tidal creek or pond, then do a second circuit an hour later, the bite is much slower. Likewise if another angler has been working the shorelines earlier that day, you are likely to have a slower catching day when you go over the same waters.

You are likely to feel taps or gentle strikes or even see the fish following your lure through the water. Pickerel are curious and often nip at a bait or lure. Although sometimes you feel a clear strike, you may also feel just a gentle tap (braided line and light or ultralight rods make this more evident) or even just an increase in weight on the line. Sometimes that means you snagged a leaf or twig, but often the extra weight means you have a toothy visitor. Frequently the pickerel pick up the lure or minnow in their mouth and hold it there without clamping down hard. When you begin reeling, you will feel weight or get a quick head shake. In a few seconds, the pickerel loses interest, opens its mouth, and releases the lure or minnow undamaged. For every fish I catch, I get perhaps three to five cases of "grab and release". It is worth casting back to the same spot again -- maybe the fish will bite harder the next time.

Once you catch a pickerel you need to unhook and release it. Pickerel have a large mouth with lots of intimidating teeth. Here is the approach I use. I wind the fish in until just a few feet of line are off the rod tip. I grab the leader and swing the fish into the boat. I grab the pickerel around its body just behind the gill area (don't touch the gills themselves) to secure the fish. Most of the pickerel I catch have the hook on the outside of their mouths. Once you are holding the fish, you can use your fingers or pliers to remove the hook quickly. You can measure and photograph the fish if desired, then slide the fish back into the water.

A small percentage of the pickerel I catch each winter are hooked with the lure inside their mouth (not deep inside their throat, but in an area where the lure cannot be easily extracted without harming the fish). Virgil Poe showed me a simple jaw spreader tool that can save a pickerel's life. The spring mechanism on the jaw spreader holds the jaws open so a lure can be removed easily without excessive prodding and grabbing with pliers.

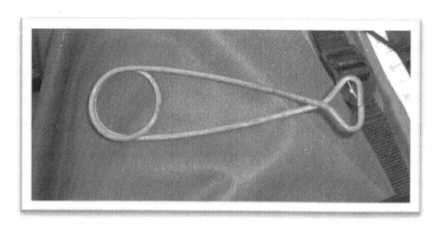

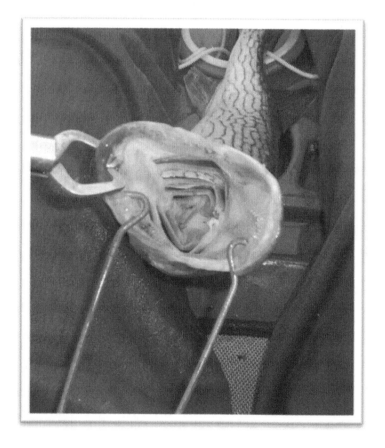

Here are some shots of the OGWLF members while pickerel fishing. The first photo shows Mark Bange with a fine pickerel.

The next photo shows the youngest OGWLF member Bruce Kellman (he is not yet an old guy, but has a work schedule that allows him to fish with the retired guys during the week).

Photo Credit: Bruce Kellman

I remember a morning last fall when Bruce asked me for some tips on catching pickerel – he had never tried for that species before. I offered some basic suggestions. Half an hour later, he reported over the VHF radio that he had caught a 24" (citation-sized) pickerel right away. It took me 8 years and nearly 1,000 pickerel before I got my first citation. Bruce is off to a great start.

Harry Steiner, another OGWLF member, joined me to fish for pickerel in a Severn River tidal creek last October.

While I was catching pickerel along the shoreline, Harry found a few active stripers just 50' from the shoreline. He cast paddletails to them and caught several of them while I watched.

Chapter 8 – Jigging Methods

Jigging is an ancient technique in which a weighted lure is lowered in the water and raised and lowered. As the lure drops, it generally flutters in a way that may simulate a wounded baitfish. Predators grab the lure on the drop or as it begins to move upward again.

<u>My Approach to Jigging</u>

In the portions of the Chesapeake Bay where I typically fish, the most commonly used jigging method is called light tackle jigging (LTJ). The species usually targeted by LTJ are stripers and sometimes bluefish. In earlier decades when weakfish (grey trout) were more prevalent in the Chesapeake, jigging was used to catch them too.

Equipment: The two rods I use for jigging are medium heavy spinning rods of about 6'2" long and Shimano Stradic 3000 reels. The spool is filled with 20-pound braid and attached to a 25-pound mono leader. I use a double-uni knot to connect line to leader. When I am jigging with jigheads and soft plastics, I use a loop knot to connect the leader to the lure. When I jig with metal lures like Stingsilvers, I often tie the leader to a heavy snap swivel using a Palomar knot and clip the lure to the snap swivel.

Many of the more experienced LTJ fisherman in the region prefer to use baitcasting tackle, in part because they believe it is easier to let out more line if the boat drifts to deeper water depths. As I noted before, I do not own or use baitcasting gear. I use my spinning tackle and have no trouble adjusting the amount of line I let out.

Lures: I use jigheads and plastics or metal lures. When using metal lures, I typically start with a 2-ounce Stingsilver or similar lure with a J-hook wrapped with hair. The lure shown below has been used hard and caught plenty of fish.

I often tie on a fly, small bucktail, or feather jig on a 12" leader just above the line/leader knot to make a tandem jigging setup. This rigging technique was described in Chapter 4 with two photos.

If the fish are biting well, I enjoy experimenting by using the other metal lures in my tackle box to see if the fish are interested in different weights and lure profiles.

The other lures I use are jigheads of ¾-ounce to 2-ounce attached to soft plastic jerkbaits. These are the mainstay of LTJ fishermen. The next photo shows the jighead and 6" BKD I used to jig on a debris pile in the Severn River in December 2012.

The second photo shows the fat 26" striper I caught with that rig. It is my largest LTJ striper caught from the kayak. I note that the leader-to-lure knot in that 2012 photo is snugged tight to the lure. I did not start using the loop knot until the following season.

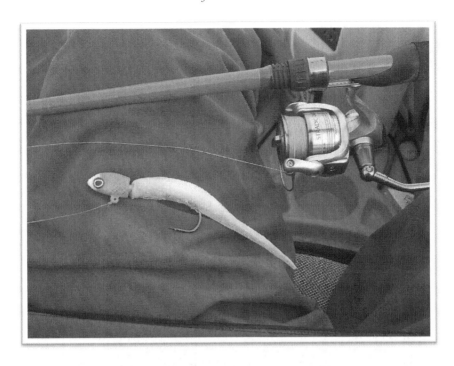

Jigging Method: The LTJ system is a popular Chesapeake Bay fishing technique that allows anglers to hook and fight large fish on light tackle. The LTJ technique has been described in great detail in Shawn Kimbro's fishing books and blog columns. He and his fishing buddies practice LTJ many times each year and have been quite successful using that method.

I enjoy LTJ but do not fish in that way as often as many other Chesapeake light tackle fishermen do. My own LTJ success is usually much more modest. I catch a few stripers or bluefish when jigging, but rarely are they larger than 24". I did have an outstanding day in early January 2016 fishing with Capt. Walleye Pete Dahlberg in the lower Chesapeake Bay. Scott Taylor and I caught dozens of fish from the low-20"s to the mid-30"s that day jigging in water from 40' to 60' while jigging both the metal and plastic lures. The photo shows Scott holding one of the large stripers he caught that day.

The basic approach to LTJ is to choose a lure heavy enough so you can feel the lure hit the bottom. The rod tip is lifted (sharply or moderately, depending on each angler's personal technique) causing the lure to lift up several feet in the water column. As the lure drops back to the bottom, lower the rod tip at a controlled rate that allows the lure to flutter but still gives enough contact with the line that you can feel a tap or change in drop rate. Sometimes a bite can be felt on the drop -- other times the bite is detected when you raise the rod tip again and feel resistance. Experienced LTJ fishermen develop a finely-tuned touch to anticipating and feeling the slightest change in lure drop rate, which is the first indicator of a bite.

Sometimes when jigging, the hook gets caught on the leader (left) or on the tail of the plastic lure itself (right) as shown below. It is surprisingly easy to feel the difference in resistance when your lure gets caught up. Once that happens, it is necessary to reel the lure in and reset it.

Most often LTJ is used to catch fish near the bottom. By watching your fishfinder, you can tell if the fish are hanging near the bottom or are suspended. When they are not on the bottom, the LTJ technique works well by jigging through the depth zones where the fish are located.

In this screen shot from October 2013, fish are thick from about 40' to the bottom near the Bay Bridge. I successfully jigged up stripers that day, including two that were invited home for dinner.

Many of the more successful LTJ practitioners are very particular about the rods, reels, braided line, leader, and lures they use. Many of these guys like to customize their jigheads by painting them with more than one color and adding eyes. They often dip the plastic jerkbaits into scented dyes to add a contrasting color. Sometimes rattles are inserted in the plastic to add sound to the lure.

Other Jigging Techniques I Have Used

The principle of jigging can be used to fish in different depths and for other species. I offer two examples at the opposite ends of the tackle weight scale. One of the ways I fish in Tampa Bay with guide Neil Taylor is to jig very small lures next to bridge pilings. He uses medium spinning rods and ties both a light Silly Willy jig (lead head molded in a banana shape) and a second hook tied with bucktail on the same loop knot.

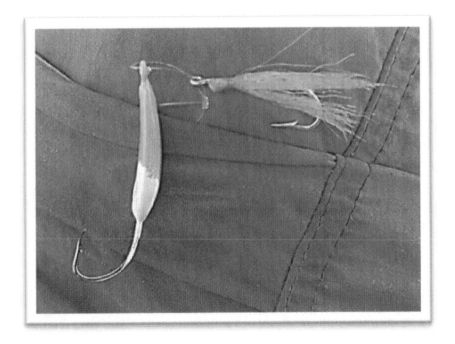

These are jigged in 10' to 15' water depth as close to pilings as possible while being bounced around by waves in a kayak. I have caught pompano (next photo) and jacks using that method.

On one day I hooked five large black drum estimated at more than 50 pounds each on that small lure. The drum were so strong that they towed the kayak around and broke off the line on barnacles on the pilings. I have watched Neil catch cobia using the same technique.

At the opposite weight extreme of the jigging scale, I jigged for halibut and ling cod in Alaska using heavy trolling rods and reels, 16-ounce and 24-oz jigheads, and massive twister tails.

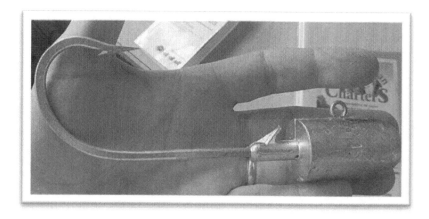

This was done while bracing against the railing of a boat in large swells. We tried to reach bottom in over 100' depth and with strong current. Within a few minutes of jigging that heavy gear my arms were sore and I got tendinitis in my elbow.

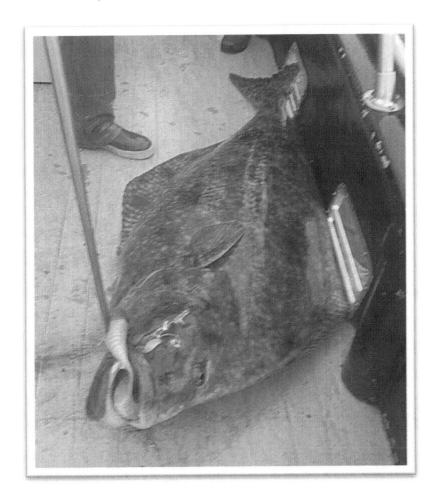

Later in the trip we downsized to 3-ounce and 4-ounce jigheads to jig for different species of Pacific rockfish with spinning tackle. I enjoyed that style of jigging better (plus it did not hurt my arms and elbows as much). I caught the large fish in the next photo using my own 7' medium travel rod that I had brought with me.

Chapter 9 – Trolling Methods

Trolling involves dragging lures behind a boat. Often multiple rods are trolled at the same time, presenting more lures to the fish. When trolling, the boat moves constantly, and the lures are able to cover a lot of water. Trolling is a very successful method for catching fish.

Introduction to Light Tackle Trolling

Earlier in the book, I explained that heavy tackle trolling in the Chesapeake Bay or offshore is outside of my fishing comfort zone. Having said that, I do enjoy light tackle trolling (LTT) from my kayak. Those methods allow me to catch many fish and watch the rods start shaking after a hard strike within three feet of where I am sitting. I find it quite exciting. In this section, I describe the light tackle style of trolling and how I do it. I do not discuss heavy tackle trolling.

Before moving into the discussion of how I practice LTT, I want to highlight the excellent book "Light Tackle Kayak Trolling the Chesapeake Bay" by Alan Battista. Alan goes into great detail on: choosing and rigging a kayak for trolling, the types of tackle and lures he prefers, how to select water bodies and routes for trolling, among other topics. I recommend Alan's book to other kayak anglers who want to learn more about the method. Alan and I developed our LTT approaches independently over many years. It is not surprising that we take slight different approaches to how we practice LTT. We both are successful using our own preferred LTT methods. I encourage readers to learn from both of us and decide which elements of LTT fall within your personal fishing comfort zone.

Equipment: I use 6' to 7' spinning rods for my trolling. At times of the year when I anticipate that larger fish are around, I use medium and medium heavy rods. In the rest of the year, I leave the medium heavy tackle at home and bring medium and medium light tackle. Most of the time I troll four rods from my kayak, unless I am in my paddle-powered kayak that has fewer rod holders.

With those rods I use Shimano Stradic 2500 or 3000 spinning reels. The spool is filled with 20-pound braid and attached to a 25-pound mono leader. I use a double-uni knot to connect line to leader and a loop knot to connect the leader to the lure. After switching from a Palomar knot to the loop knot in 2013, I noticed that my catch rate increased. I cannot be sure if the loop knot was the main factor in the improvement – but it certainly helped.

Other light tackle trollers may choose longer and/or heavier rods, especially if they troll lures with strong water resistance, like umbrella rigs or large diving crankbaits. That is personal preference – there is no right or wrong answer.

I actually troll with even lighter tackle on some occasions. In November 2015, I did a combination pickerel casting and striper trolling trip in my kayak in the Severn River. I carried an ultralight, a light, a medium light, and a medium rod. I caught a few pickerel using the ultralight and light rods. Then I trolled in the mouth of a tidal creek using all four rods and caught stripers on each rod, including a 19" striper on the ultralight rod. That rod was not designed for trolling and catching fish of that size. But it performed admirably when deployed in that way.

Lures: Nearly all the lures I use for trolling are jigheads or bucktails with paddletails. Sometimes I add a Gulp twister tail to the spread. These lures are great for trolling because their shape allows the lure to swim without having to constantly twitch or work the rod. During most of the year when I am trolling in water shallower than 10', I use 3/8-ounce to 3/4-ounce jigheads or bucktails with plastic tails. In other locations I troll in deeper water and use up to 1.5-ounce jigheads or bucktails to get the lure deeper.

My go-to plastic tail is the 12 Fathom 3" Fat Sam mullet. It swims with a seductive motion at slow, medium, and fast trolling speeds. Stripers love that lure during much of the year. During late spring when larger stripers enter the Severn River, I often increase the size of the paddletails to 4" or 5". A lure that has worked well for me during that period is the 4.5" Offshore Angler Saltwater Sally from Bass Pro Shops. I also troll with 4" to 6" swim shads on some spring trips. Some examples of my trolling lures are shown in the next few photos.

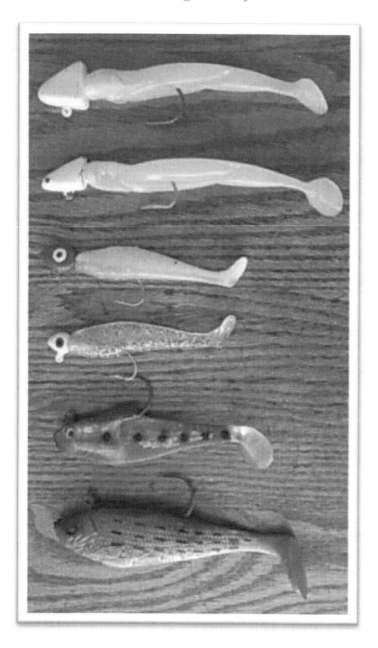

The colors I usually choose are the same as the ones I like for casting - white, chartreuse, gold, silver, tan, clear, or similar colors. But on some days other colors like electric chicken, blue, brown, and black get lots of attention.

When bluefish show up, I lose some plastic tails. At that point I switch plastics to the stretchier varieties like the Z-Man tails or add a small metal spoon to one or more rods in the spread.

Alan Battista likes to target stripers suspended in deeper waters. He often uses large swimming plugs and diving crankbaits. Even though they are very effective for him, I choose not to use crankbaits as I stated previously. He also uses different types of umbrella rigs that have rigid wires separating multiple baits. He developed his own version of a small umbrella he calls the "Chesapeake Rig". These are bulkier and heavier lures than what I prefer to use. Even though they do catch many stripers for Alan and other kayak anglers, they are outside my comfort zone.

The LTT Method

My LTT Evolution: Let me start by explaining my earliest LTT methods. Years ago I found that when I was chasing breaking fish and birds in my boat, the birds had often moved to another spot by the time I got to the spot where I had seen them. I tried casting for the fish, but did not always find the right location. To help me determine where feeding fish could be found within a general area, I decided to troll with the same rods and lures that I was casting to those fish. I cast out two small lures, stuck the rods in the rear rod holders, and usually within a few minutes I was able to locate a school of fish. At that point I could continue trolling or could stop and cast to them. I still follow this approach a few times each year.

As I got interested in kayak fishing 15 years ago, I often paddled from one perch-casting spot to another. I decided to try trolling the same light lures and rods in between casting spots. I caught a few small stripers but did not have very much success. But I liked the concept of keeping a few lures in play for most of the time I was on the water.

On a hot summer day in 2011, I tried a technique I call ultralight tackle trolling (ULTT). I was casting to shorelines for perch without much success. I eventually got to a stretch of shoreline that always looks fishy, but which typically does not produce well using casted lures. I decided to troll very slowly (~1 mph) through this area with three ultralight rods using several different types of small lures. My normal paddling rate would have been much too fast. I had to use a paddling cadence of stroke/stroke/gliiiiiiiide, to keep the lures moving slowly. This cadence allowed the lures to move up gently in the water column during the stroke portion and to drop in the water column during the glide portion.

All three rods caught perch that day. All of the lures I used were small and had either a paddle tail or a spinner blade, or both. I made a bunch of passes along the same 75-yard stretch of shoreline and caught perch almost every time. Apparently, the fish in that region preferred a slow trolled lure to one that was cast out and retrieved. I stayed as close to the shore as I could but far enough out to avoid sunken tree branches.

Among my earliest trolling efforts for larger fish was my first visit to the Susquehanna Flats in the spring of 2012. Historically during April striped bass congregate by the millions at the very head end of the Chesapeake Bay in an area known as the Susquehanna Flats. The Susquehanna River is the largest tributary to the Chesapeake. As it enters the northern bay, it has created a broad shallow area with very low salinity.

I launched from a marina in Havre de Grace, MD and paddled out to the open waters without having a strong game plan. As soon as the water depth reached 5', I set out two rods with a paddletail and a swim shad.

In just a few minutes, I had a 21" striper on board. Over the next four hours I caught numerous stripers to 24" using LTT in depths less than 10'. Not only were the fish hooked – I was too!

I trolled some during the summer of 2012. The following spring, I returned to the Flats. I trolled in much the same locations I had during 2012. This time I found no stripers but did catch four big largemouth bass and one large carp that hit a trolled swim shad in 4' water depth. I had not realized that carp would hit a trolled lure. It was exciting to wind in a strong carp in shallow water.

I enjoyed the shallow-water, light tackle style of trolling I used at the Flats but preferred to find a fishing spot closer to home. I looked at the marine charts and decided to try trolling in shallow water near the mouth of my home waters -- the Severn River. On my first visit there, I trolled in the 5' to 6' depth range. I found one area about the size of a tennis court that held 15" to 16" stripers. Each time I made a pass by that spot, one of the rods went down. I ended up catching 8 stripers of about the same size, and all were taken in the same small area.

That first Severn trolling trip was not highly productive, but it proved that my concept was sound. The next week I launched from a different launch point. As I paddled from the launch to the river mouth, I set out my trolling rods to see what else I might find. To my delight, part way to the river mouth I had a good strike and wound in a 21" striper. I decided to work that area for a while and began paddling 200-yard passes across the same area. On the second pass, one rod went down hard. It turned out to be another 21" fish. Over the next 20 minutes, I hooked two 15" and one 19" striper. Then 20 minutes later, a powerful 23" fish hit the lure.

I continued working the area for another half hour without any more takers. I then took off on a long paddle to explore more areas, without success. On my way back to the ramp, I made one more pass through the zone where the other fish had hit. The rod with a 6" swim shad began shaking vigorously, with line pulling out against the drag. I stopped paddling and tried to stop the initial run. In the meantime, the fish began swimming back and forth, spinning the kayak and threatening to tangle all three lines. Five minutes later, I hauled a tired 26" striper onboard. That was my largest fish of the year from the kayak and gave me a great fight on a medium spinning rod.

Trolling remained productive for about three weeks during the spring of 2013 then the larger fish left the river. From late summer through October that year I often trolled in the Severn parallel to the shoreline just one cast length from the shore. Typical water depths were 2' to 5'. I caught numerous stripers from 18" to 22" during that time. During the late summer, I often trolled two small spinners and two larger paddletails at the same time. 90% of the fish caught on the spinners were perch, and 90% of the fish caught on the paddletails were rockfish.

One downside to LTT from a paddle-powered kayak is that the steady paddling for 4-5 hours wreaked havoc on my old shoulder joints. The following winter I purchased a Native Watercraft Slayer Propel 13 pedal-powered kayak that allowed me to keep moving with the pedals and steering with the rudder while reeling in fish. This made trolling much easier and caused me to make many more LTT trips from that point forward.

During the 2014 and 2015 seasons, I found large stripers in the Severn River for three weeks during May. Neither year brought good trolling success in the river throughout the summer or fall. However, during the fall of 2015, a nor'easter storm trapped bait in the upper reaches of a Severn tributary. I trolled that area nine days in a row (often in wind and rain) and caught over 120 stripers up to 27". I used my 11' paddle kayak and trolled two rods during those trips.

In addition to making many LTT trips in the Severn, I enjoyed exploring various shallow water spots to the south of Kent Narrows from July to October. My usual strategy there involved trolling four rods in water depths from 3' to 4'. I followed grassy shorelines keeping a close watch on my fishfinder to make sure I remained in the target depth zones. On a day with low water levels I needed to reposition my trolling route farther from the shore to keep within my target depth range. When I got bites, I looked at my GPS tracks then circled back and trolled through the same areas repeatedly.

<u>My Rigging and Fishing Methods for LTT from a Kayak</u>

The following sections give more specific information about how I practice LTT in my kayaks.

Number of Rods, Locations, and Rigging: My paddle-powered Manta Ray 11 kayak has an adjustable Scotty rod holder on either side in the gear track in front of the seat area. I rotate them out 45 degrees to the front and use a 6' or 6'6" spinning rod in each holder. I currently troll two rods from that kayak, but plan to add more rod holders for 2016.

The Scotty rod holders I use come with a rubber strap that can fasten over the top and keep the rod from sliding out. In theory this is a sound concept. But in practice, when a fish begins shaking the rod, it is difficult to get the strap unhooked. I removed the strap from all of my rod holders. Some anglers may be concerned that without a strap a strong fish could pull the rod out of the rod holder. While that may be possible, it has not happened to me. I keep my drags loose (I can pull line off the spool with my hand using a moderate tug). Any strong lunge by the fish would take line rather than the entire rod. Further, the sizes of rods I use all bend somewhat under strain. The force of a fish on the hook causes the rod butt to get wedged against the plastic of the rod holders. On large fish, I sometimes have a difficult time removing the rod from the holder due to the pressure of the butt against the plastic.

My pedal-powered kayak has two rod holders in front of my seat and two behind the seat allowing me to troll four rods. I rotate the rear holders out 45 degrees to the rear. The two rod holders in the front must be offset to the sides so the rod butts do not interfere with the pedaling motion. I added Scotty extenders between the bases and the rod holders.

I put the two heavier rods in the rear and use heavier jigheads on those lines. In the front I use lighter rods and smaller/lighter lures. Nearly all the lures I use in LTT are paddletails with an occasional Gulp twister tail. I normally use a variety of weights, colors, and lure shapes on my 4-rod spread. On some days, one of the lures clearly outcatches all the others. Once you learn that, you can put that same lure on a second or third rod. On other days, all the lures seem to catch equally well. It pays to give the fish a choice to see what they prefer that day.

I do not use lures that tend to move in different directions when being trolled – for example, diving crankbaits. If I did decide to use that type of lure, I would reduce the number of rods to two.

I do not have a precise method for letting line out to specified distances – I don't think it is necessary for the places I fish. Instead I toss the front lures out with a gentle flip and the rear lines with a longer toss. The rods are placed in the rod holders, and I begin pedaling or paddling. The next photo shows me trolling four lines along a grassy shoreline near Kent Narrows.

Photo Credit: Mark Bange

Trolling Plans and Patterns: I find it is useful to start out each trip with a mental trolling plan (direction, depth, distance, etc.). Most of my trolling is done in shallow water (less than 10') and often in depths less than 5'. When I am trolling in shallow depths, I use small jigheads (3/8-ounce to 3/4-ounce) or bucktails. I try to work the same routes each time I fish in an area to see if fish are there and where they may be clustered. Wind speed and direction can create sheltered areas and rough areas. I try to consider wind and tidal currents when making my trip plan, but often actual conditions on the water do not match the predictions.

When I catch fish in a location, I often circle around and troll through the same area again. I keep repeating this until I stop getting bites. The tracks on my GPS screen are very useful for this type of precision navigation. I have a pretty good memory and can remember many of the hundreds of spots where I have hooked fish in the past. To augment my memory, particularly when trolling in a new location, I can mark waypoints on the GPS screen.

While trolling, I usually use the split screen setting on my fishfinder/GPS so I can follow a similar track each time while still watching for fish on the sonar part of the screen. The next screen shot was taken during one of my first Severn River trolling trips. I caught a fish then made numerous parallel 200-yard runs upriver and downriver past the same location. The depth varied from 7' to about 13' depending on how close I was to the shoreline.

In most of my shallow water trolling trips, I rarely see fish arches or bait clusters on the fishfinder screen. Nevertheless, by using the GPS tracks to stay in a productive area I am able to catch many fish.

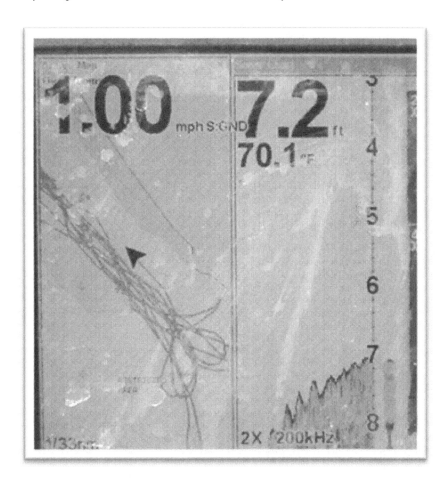

The following screen shot shows my trolling pattern in a spot with slightly deeper water. After catching my first fish, I trolled in all directions around a central spot to look for more fish. I caught many fish that day, but they were scattered throughout the several-acre area and did not show up on the fishfinder.

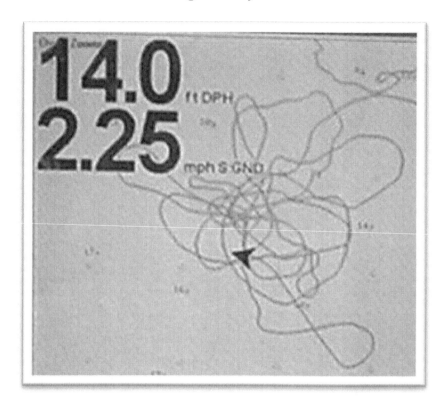

On that day, I caught more than 20 stripers from that area with the largest at 27.5".

Although I rely heavily on my electronics, Terry Hill, one of the OGWLF members, has not installed any electronics on his kayak. Yet he continues to be very successful catching stripers by LTT. He seems to have an innate knack for finding fish whether fishing from his paddle-powered Raptor kayak (below) or his pedal-powered Hobie kayak.

Photo Credit: Mark Bange

On some trips the fish are not biting where I think they should be, or the water conditions are undesirable (bad water clarity or color, floating leaves or grasses, too windy). When that happens, I follow several options:

- I can keep trolling in those locations in the hope that the fish will begin biting as the current movement changes.

- I can move on to other nearby areas that have similar habitats, but which may have more desirable conditions.

- I can push my trolling pattern out to slightly deeper water (5' to 10').

- I can focus on certain structures that offer either shelter or a moving current. Take for example the large concrete and rock breakwater slightly south of Kent Narrows. As tidal currents push lots of water north or south, the water hits the breakwater and deflects off of both ends. Water depths range from less than 5' to more than 25'. Fish may seek out baitfish trapped near the wall or in eddies spun off the ends. I often troll along the breakwater but the bite is inconsistent, and the hot spots move around from day-to-day and even from hour-to-hour as the current velocity and directions changes with the tidal cycle.

All of those strategies worked for me last summer. In many cases, when I explored new areas adjacent to my normal spots, I found fish. Not all of these spots worked well, but I was able to find a few new places to add to my trolling patterns. I also found some spots that were sheltered on a northerly wind and others that were good on a southerly wind. Likewise, I found some spots that were very good under higher water conditions but were tough for trolling under low water.

By visiting the same areas repeatedly under different wind and water level conditions, I learned how to work the areas effectively and where fish tended to be found under different conditions and at different times of the year. This knowledge provided more trip planning options and helped me develop a good shallow water LTT comfort zone.

The next photo shows OGWLF member John Rentch holding up a beautiful striper he caught near the mouth of Baltimore Harbor in October 2015. Four of the OGWLF members spent the morning trolling for stripers from our kayaks. We all did well, but John's fish was about the largest. We teased him that the angle of the photo made it look like his fishing rod was still smoking from all the fish he caught.

Trolling Speed and Direction: There are different opinions about how fast to troll and how to troll in relation to the current flow. Here are some of my observations on those subjects.

I watch the speed on my GPS closely and try to troll in the range of about 2.5 to 3.5 knots. I catch most of my fish at those speeds. One important thing to consider is whether you are measuring speed through the water (typically measured by a paddle wheel sensor) or speed over ground. My GPS is set to display speed over ground. Depending on the forces of wind and current, your speed over ground will be different if you are moving

Photo Credit: Mark Bange

down current (faster speed) or up current (slower). Assume a current flow of 0.5 knots. A down-current speed of 3.5 knots over ground is the same as an up-current speed of 2.5 knots over ground in terms of actual speed through water.

Part of trolling success is putting the lures at the depth where the fish are. Because of the relatively light lures I use, I am targeting fish swimming in the top few feet of the water column, regardless of the actual water depth. Alan Battista's book describes his efforts to use heavier lures or deep-diving crankbaits to target fish at deeper depths in the water column. A good fishfinder is helpful in learning the depth at which your target fish are located.

Another element of trolling success is moving the lure at a speed that makes it look at least somewhat like a food item. On a good day when the fish are abundant and hungry, this does not need to be precise -- the fish will hear or sense the lure coming and will seek it out. On other days when the bite is slower, you must do your best to get a realistic-looking lure in their faces.

If you are trolling in shallow water, you need to maintain enough speed so the lure does not hit bottom. Or you can reduce the weight of the lure. On the other hand, if you are trolling a lure that has an enticing swimming motion, going too slow or too fast may change the way the lure runs. I try to watch my FF/GPS closely to see the instantaneous depth and speed. If I am trolling in 3.5' depth and I come to a point where the bottom rises to 2.8', I either veer toward deeper water or increase my speed, which lifts the lure in the water column.

If you are using a new lure, hold the lure in the water next to the boat and see how it swims at different speeds (i.e., your paddle or pedal rate). That can help a lot in making the lure look realistic. A GPS is helpful in monitoring your speed. The paddletail styles I use have a wide speed range under which they swim well.

In general, fishing often improves when the water is moving from a tidal current. Some people believe that the best trolling comes when the lures are moving in the same direction as the current. I have had some days when the trolling is clearly more productive when the lures are moving with the current. Yet on other days the bite is equally good whether the lures are moving with the current, against the current, or across the current.

When trolling in shallow water near a shoreline, I feel that I am targeting stripers that are scattered around a general area. They will sense the lures moving in their vicinity and if interested, they will strike, regardless of the movement of the lures vs. the current direction. If I am targeting a piece of structure (piling, concrete wall, rock pile, or grassy point sticking out into the current) I find that the fish are more likely to be oriented in a way that brings the bait to them. If you are trolling near structure, try dragging the lures past the structure from different directions to see which direction gets the most interest.

I recommend that you not worry too much about the speed you use for kayak trolling -- the fish can catch up to your lure at any reasonable speed you are moving in a kayak.

Lure Appearance: Several things can keep a lure from swimming well or looking natural. When the lure does not look like a food item or is swimming in an unnatural way, predators are less likely to strike the lure. This is true for all types of fishing. When casting, the angler retrieves the lure frequently and can quickly see if the lure looks odd. But when trolling, the angler is often unaware that the lure is not swimming well. It requires intentional effort to check the lures periodically to make sure they still look and swim correctly.

If the lure bumps bottom it often picks up grass, slime, shell, or other debris. If the water surface has much floating grass, leaves, or other debris, your lures are likely to snag the materials making the lures look unrealistic and keeping the paddletail from swinging in its normal rhythm.

When bluefish are in the area, you may feel a tap or a hard strike, but the fish does not remain on the hook. Often that signifies that the tail of the lure has been bitten off.

In other cases, a fish strikes the lure but does not hook up. Sometimes, the plastic tail slides down the hook leaving the lure looking unattractive to a fish. I call this action "pulling down its pants".

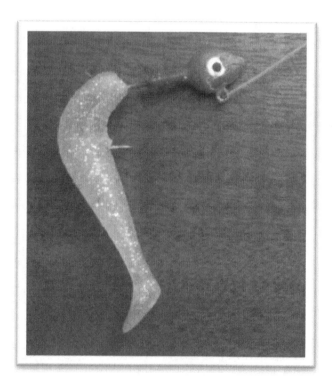

Most paddletails are designed to swim smoothly in an upright orientation. When attaching paddletails or other soft plastic tails to jigheads or bucktails, it is very important to have the hook point enter and exit along the midline (bottom lure in photo). I have seen many beginners run the hook point through the nose of a soft plastic lure but pull it out through the side rather than the top of the lure (top lure in the photo). A soft plastic tail rigged that way or in some other unbalanced manner will not swim naturally and generally gets less attention from the predators.

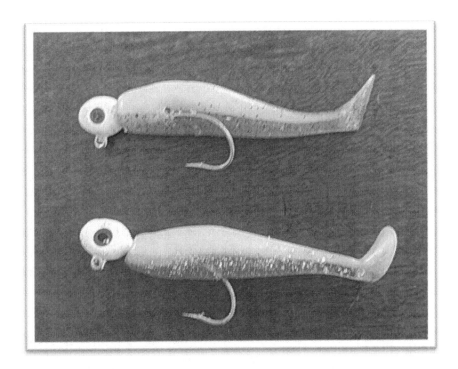

Under any of these conditions, be prepared to check your lures frequently to keep them clean. Otherwise you have unproductive lures in your spread.

Catching and Unhooking a Fish While Underway: Many anglers seem surprised that I am able to troll four lines at a time from my kayaks. I have been trolling this way for the past few years and don't think much about it anymore. To avoid regular tangles between lines, there are several things to keep in mind:

- Keep moving forward as much of the time as possible, even when you have a fish on the line. If the kayak continues forward in more or less a straight direction, the lines will trail behind the kayak and maintain their spacing. This is much easier to do when using a pedal-powered kayak. I recall days of trolling four lines from my paddle-powered kayaks. When I got a fish on one of the lines, I had to stop paddling to wind it in. If I had been heading into the wind or waves when I stop paddling, the kayak quickly stopped its forward momentum and turned down-wind or down-current, leaving the other lines bowed out and crossing. If smaller fish were involved, I could get them in quickly and turn the kayak. With larger fish, I took my time to get the fish onboard then sorted out any tangled lines. The number of times I had major tangles turned out to be relatively few.

- Put your heavier lures in the rear and farther back. This allows the lures on the rear lines to sink more quickly and minimize contact with the front lines.

- When making turns, try to turn as gradually as possible. The lines on the inside of the turn tend to drop in the water column and get some slack, whereas the lines on the outside of the turn tend to rise up.

Most of my trolling is done in my pedal-powered kayak. When I hook a fish while trolling, I try to keep pedaling. If there is some structure or shallow depth nearby that could cause some navigation or tangling issues, I turn gradually away from it. I bring the fish in as quickly as possible. If the fish is below 18", I generally release it quickly by shaking it from the barbless hooks. If it is larger and I want to take a photo, I orient the kayak in the downwind or down-current direction to allow the lines to trail out behind the kayak as I drift. I have my measuring board (Hawg Trough) handy and get my photo quickly. Then I return the fish to the water (I do not keep fish caught on my kayak). If I have stopped pedaling, I need to wind in all of the other lines and check them for dirt or debris.

If I do catch a large, strong fish while trolling, it may try to swim around on various sides of the kayak and can easily cross other lines. I rationalize this as being a good problem to have. For most of us, our goal is to catch large fish. If I do catch a large fish, I am willing to spend a few minutes afterwards untangling lines, if necessary.

In May 2015, I trolled paddletails and swim shads for large bluefish near the mouth of Delaware Bay. On three occasions, I hooked two of them at once. My strategy then was to loosen the drag on the first rod and set it in a rod holder. I then fought the second fish to the boat and released it. When that was done, I went back to work on the first fish. It was pretty exciting to be pulled around by two 36" bluefish in a 10' kayak.

Chapter 10 – Methods for Fishing with Bait

One of the oldest and most successful ways to catch fish is to toss a baited hook into the water and wait for a fish to eat it. Bait fishing can be done with various rigs, different types of live or dead bait, and in different environments. I do not fish often these days with bait. Lenny Rudow's "Fishing in the Chesapeake" offers more information about bait fishing. Interested readers are referred to that book. In this chapter, I give brief summaries of several types of bait fishing and bit more detail on actual catches I have made using bait.

<u>Bait Fishing Methods I Have Tried and Do Not Use Any Longer</u>

Floating Bait under a Bobber: In this simple technique, some type of live or dead bait is attached to a hook. Some of the common types of bait used are earthworms, bloodworms, and grass shrimp. The hook is suspended in the water column by attaching it to a floating bobber. When a fish grabs the bait, the bobber is pulled forward or under the water. At that point the angler winds it in.

Some of my earliest fishing experiences involved drifting earthworms under a bobber and catching bluegills. To a young boy, that was great fun. Years later, I took some neighborhood kids to a stormwater pond and let them catch bluegills in the same manner.

I do not fish this way anymore, but I still observe shoreline fisherman catching white perch and yellow perch this way in the spring. It can be effective when the fish are schooled up and hungry.

Livelining: Livelining is a popular way of catching stripers in the Chesapeake Bay. Stripers love to eat Norfolk spot, a common bottom-dwelling fish that moves into the mid-Chesapeake in early summer.

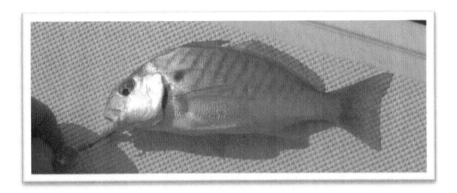

Spot can be caught by dropping small hooks tipped with pieces of bloodworm over shell bottom. Spot are unhooked and placed into a live well on the boat. When enough spot have been collected, the boat is moved to a location where large stripers are expected to be. The pilings of the Bay Bridge are a common target.

Medium or heavier power rods are rigged with large circle hooks or J-hooks. The hook is usually run through the back of the spot in front of the dorsal fin. Some liveliners hook the spot in other ways. The spot is tossed out with the drag set very light or leaving the bail open. Spot can be fished weightless or with small egg sinkers threaded on the line. The spot swim toward the bottom. The spot can sense when a striper is nearby and often begin swimming erratically. Once the striper grabs the spot, the angler waits for a few seconds, then closes the bail and sets the hook.

I recall a day in June 2013 when I fished with well-known local angler Skip Zinck on his 27' Grady White. Skip is quite skilled at livelining. We caught a bunch of spot and relocated to an area with schools of large stripers.

Skip had more anglers on board than livelining rigs that day. I volunteered to sit on the bow and try to catch fish from the same school using LTJ. The guys who livelined caught fish steadily for several hours. I was tickled that I caught the largest fish of the day (31") – and I did it with a jig and BKD rather than a live spot.

I have tried livelining a few times on my own without great success. I am unlikely to fish in this way again for stripers. Like most fishing methods, those who do their homework, optimize their tackle, and practice can become very successful at catching stripers.

Chumming: The concept of chumming is to grind up an oily fish like menhaden and broadcast a stream of small pieces that drift away from the boat with the current. The anglers bait their hooks with larger chunks of the same baitfish and allow the baited hooks to drift along with the chum slick. Fresh chum can be made on the boat if it is equipped with a meat grinder. The chunks are mixed with water to form a thin soupy stream that is ladled into the water. For those who do not have chum grinders, frozen logs or buckets of chum are available at tackle shops. These are placed in mesh bags or in containers with holes drilled in them. As the chum thaws, it dribbles out creating a down-current chum slick.

I tried chumming once on a charter boat and did not have much success with it. Both livelining and chumming fall outside of my fishing comfort zone.

Drifting Bait: Chesapeake Bay anglers often use live eels, soft crabs, peeler crabs, and clams for bait. These baits can be weighted and drifted back from the boat. I don't fish locally in this way and have no practical experience with the method.

When I fish in Tampa with guide Neil Taylor, we almost always throw soft plastic lures. In January 2014, we had a very windy and cold day that did not allow casting in open water on the flats. Neil brought some live shrimp. We paddled into a sheltered canal and anchored up a cast-length away from dock pilings. I threw shrimp on a small hook with 1 or 2 split shots to get it near the bottom. I expected that I would slowly retrieve the shrimp, but Neil told me to let it sit near a piling or under the dock. Sometimes I left it alone for 10-15 minutes at a time and kept a tight line waiting for the nibble. The bite was definitely slow that day, but I caught sheepshead, redfish, black drum, and ladyfish -- all were small. Nevertheless, on that day, bait helped to avoid a skunk.

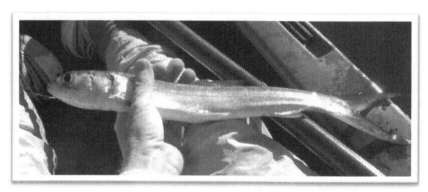

Bait Fishing Methods I Continue to Use

Casting Live Bait: In Chapter 7, I describe how I cast live minnows and retrieve them like a lure when fishing for pickerel in the coldest months of the winter. This basic approach can be used with larger baitfish in various other types of fishing. Years ago, in Louisiana, I fished with a guide and cast live shrimp behind a popping cork while fishing for speckled trout. Nearly all of my speckled trout fishing these days is done with soft plastic lures.

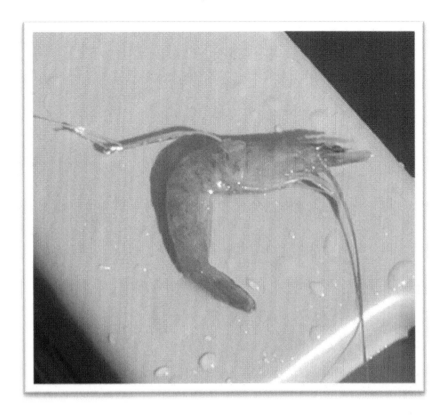

Bottom Fishing: In my earlier fishing years, I spent much of the summer drifting over hard-bottomed bars (Hackett, Tolly, and Thomas Point are examples of bars where I fished) and fishing with bottom rigs and cut bait. The most common type of bottom rig is a wire rig with two arms. The one shown below is about 24" long. Hooks with leaders are added to each arm. A weight is clipped on the bottom. Bait (often bloodworms, shrimp, squid, or peeler crab) is threaded onto each hook.

I also have used a product called Fishbites in the bloodworm flavor. Fishbites are thin strips of scented and flavored material on a mesh backing. They slowly dissolve in the water sending out a scent cloud. Live bloodworms are perishable and cannot be kept for more than a few days between trips. Fishbites can be kept in your tackle box for months and are useful to have on hand as a spare. I found that they produce a comparable bite to live bloodworms when the water temperature rises sufficiently to disperse the scent cloud. For the mid-Chesapeake region where I live, that usually occurs in early June.

The rigs are dropped to the bottom. Some anglers tie their own rigs with mono line and minimize the amount of metal hardware on the rig.

In my early fishing years, I used snelled J-hooks on the bottom rigs. These caught fish, but had a tendency to get swallowed by the fish more often than I liked. About 25 years ago, while on vacation in the Outer Banks of North Carolina, I discovered small, thin-wire circle hooks with tiny spinner blades. I began using this style of snelled hooks on my bottom rigs and had less deep hooking problems. They easily catch small and medium fish and do not require the angler to set the hook. I often fished several rods at once by setting the rods in rod holders and waiting for the bite.

The next photo shows three types of leadered hooks I have used on bottom rigs. The style I use most often is the small circle hook on the left.

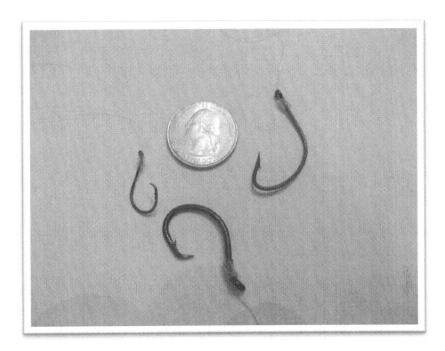

Last September I caught a 36" sandbar shark on one of these small circle hooks baited with a chunk of frozen shrimp while targeting small weakfish and speckled trout. If I were intentionally targeting sharks, I would have used much heavier tackle. But the results show the versatility of the simple bottom rig.

Photo Credit: John Rentch

The larger circle hook in the bottom of the hook photo is used when targeting somewhat larger fish. In 2012 I made several trips to Mattawoman Creek to target blue catfish. I bottom fished using the larger circle hooks and earthworm or cut menhaden for bait. I caught several catfish to about 24".

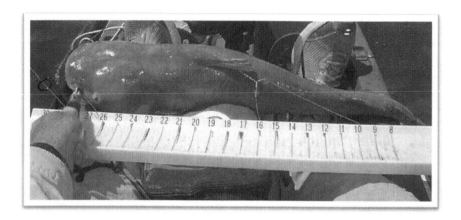

The hook on the right in the hook photo is a flounder hook with a slightly different shape. If I am targeting flounder, I use that style hook.

I make up several of these rigs in advance, shove the hook points into a cork, and store them in one quart slide-lock bags. This minimizes tangling and speeds up rigging when I am on the water.

In past years when I tried some surf fishing, I used the same type of bottom rig with my surf rod. I have not tried surf fishing in many years and no longer own surf casting gear.

Another common type of bottom rig does not use the rigid double-hook wire frame. Instead, a sliding "fishfinder rig" is threaded on the line and a single hook is tied on the end. The fishfinder rig holds the sinker and allows the line to move easily through a hollow sleeve. When a fish takes the bait, it can swim off without feeling the weight of the sinker.

I have not used fishfinder rigs often, but was advised by a tackle shop on the Eastern Shore of Virginia last September to use an oversized version of this rig to target large red drum. My fishing buddy John Rentch and I rigged up several medium heavy rods with oversized fishfinder rigs, large circle hooks, and 6 ounces of weight as shown in the photo.

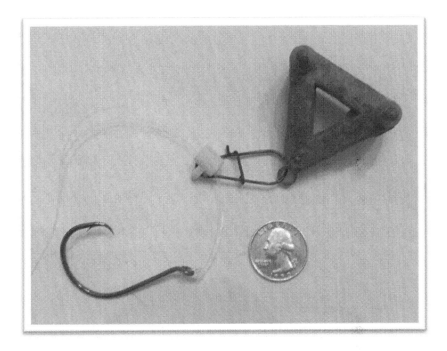

We baited up with large chunks of frozen spot. We drifted across a fishing reef and dropped the bait to the bottom with a very light drag setting. In less than a minute, a powerful fish grabbed my bait and began swimming off. I counted to ten, tightened the drag, and set the hook hard. Ten minutes later I brought a 38" redfish to the boat. This remains my personal best redfish.

Photo Credit: John Rentch

When I make my annual late summer trip to the Eastern Shore of Virginia, I spend several days bottom fishing near the Wachapreague Inlet or the CBBT. My fishing buddies and I often catch many species of fish drifting over different depths. We use live minnows, squid strips, and frozen shrimp for bait. On some days we substitute Gulp paddletails for the bait.

Flounder is a common catch, along with croaker, toadfish, sea robin, whiting, and black sea bass. Todd Kimmell, my fishing buddy and former co-worker, is shown in the next photo with a nice flounder he caught at the CBBT.

Some of the unexpected species I caught while bottom fishing in these areas include a grey triggerfish, spiny butterfly ray, and mantis shrimp.

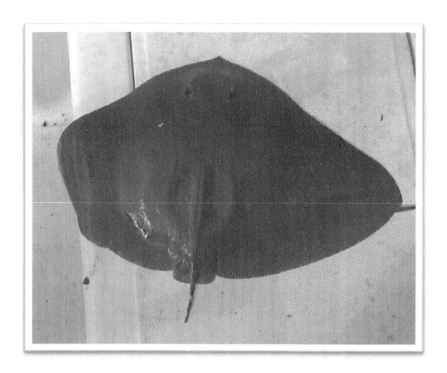

Many years ago, I fished from head boats leaving from several different ports in the Florida Keys, southeast Florida, and North Carolina. The head boats anchored over wrecks or other structure. All anglers dropped their baited hooks and hoped for a catch. One of the fun things about those trips is the great variety of species caught by the anglers on the boat – you never knew what type of fish would come up next.

My largest fish caught by bottom fishing are halibut and lingcod. I fished on a boat out of Homer, AK. We used huge circle hooks and large chunks of octopus and a sardine for bait.

The water was more than 100' deep, and the currents were strong. We typically used weights of 2 or 3 pounds to reach and hold bottom. We used heavy trolling rods and reels. Even with that stout tackle, it was hard work to bring a big fish to the surface (and to hold a heavy lingcod up for a photo).

Part Four: Fishing from a Kayak

Chapter 11 – Why Fish from a Kayak?

I fish many times each year from my kayaks. Most of the charters I have booked in recent years are with a kayak fishing guide. Kayak fishing has become a central part of my fishing comfort zone. This chapter talks about why I choose to fish from a kayak. The following chapters cover other aspects of kayak fishing, such as how to choose a kayak, what gear you need and what other gear is desirable, and how to accommodate your fishing equipment in a boat with limited storage space.

Positive Aspects about Fishing from a Kayak

Size and Weight: Kayaks are small and lightweight compared to most boats. They can be stored at home and transported using regular vehicles – powerful towing vehicles are not needed. In my community, the architectural control guidelines prohibit outside storage of boats on trailers. I was forced to find a boat that fits into my garage.

Kayaks are small enough that I can store several of them in my walkout basement. The photo shows the four kayaks I owned until last year – I now own two fishing kayaks.

I own a minivan (previously a Honda Odyssey and now a Toyota Sienna). I can use a roof rack if I am hauling more than one kayak at a time.

But I am able to fit either one of my smaller kayaks fully inside my minivan and still close the rear hatch. This makes loading and unloading simple and fast.

I can load my kayak and fishing gear into the minivan in just a few minutes. There is no need to worry about loading a large boat with gear, hitching up the trailer, and driving it to a launch point. On several occasions last summer, I finished work on the computer and checked the wind forecast. Within 30 minutes of that time, I was able to change my clothes, load the van, drive to the launch point, unload the kayak and gear, and start fishing. That logistical simplicity makes my kayaks very appealing.

Launch Locations: When using a power boat, it is necessary to find a formal launch ramp or pay for a permanent boat slip. On weekends, these ramps can be crowded. Many ramps charge a user fee. On the other hand, kayaks are light enough that they can be carried or rolled on carts or trolleys from a parking area to any open shoreline that is accessible to the public. One of the counties on the Eastern Shore of Maryland charges a ramp fee for all trailered boats, including kayaks on trailers. But small boats like kayaks that are transported without trailers can launch for free.

I prefer regular developed launch spots with dedicated parking areas, but with my lightest kayak, I am able to use other spots that are not as user-friendly. One location I like to visit each May gets me into shallow water at the headwaters of a tidal river where carp spawn at that time. I enjoy paddling in shallow water and seeing hundreds of large carp swimming just a few feet from my kayak. The closest formal launch ramp is nearly two miles away. I park on the shoulder of a road and lift my kayak over a guard rail. I slide it down a bank to get to the water. It is not optimal, but it does give me access to otherwise remote waters.

Fuel Efficiency: When I use my kayak, the only fuel I require is gas for the minivan to drive to and from my launch point. Since most of my trips are close to home, I use less than a gallon of gas for each trip. I don't need to worry about outboard oil, fuel stabilizer, or other additives.

I drive with the kayak inside the minivan, which adds no additional air resistance when driving. Even when I place a kayak on the roof racks, the incremental air drag has little impact on my fuel economy.

Exercise: I do not go to a gym or participate in other formal exercise programs. Using a kayak is great for me because I can enjoy my sport while getting a good workout. My pedal-powered kayak works out my legs, and my paddle-powered kayak works out my arms and upper body.

Stealth and Shallow Water Capability: A kayak can move very quietly as long as the user concentrates on not splashing excessively. I am able to sneak up on fish for casting and LTT that might be spooked by hearing a motor running. I attribute some of my success at pickerel fishing to being able to move quietly into areas where the pickerel can be found.

I am able to get into many spots in shallow coves or in the headwaters of creeks that would be prohibitive for a boat. A kayak floats in just a few inches of water. Persons using pedal-powered kayaks must retract their propulsion units when getting in very shallow water, but that can be done quickly. I like to fish in shallow water. Under low water conditions, I occasionally find that I will bottom out and have to stand up and drag the kayak over a sand bar or mud flat. Often it is possible to back out of these shallow spots.

Negative Aspects about Fishing from a Kayak

Limited Storage Space: Kayaks are small and have limited storage capabilities. Some kayaks offer more built in storage options than others. Most kayaks have front access to the inside of the hull.

This storage is suitable for items that need not be readily accessible, but they are not useful for tackle trays or rods that are needed throughout the trip. Some models have small storage bins built into the floor of the kayak and accessible through a hatch cover. I owned a small Malibu Mini-X kayak for about a year. It offered a storage area with a hanging bag in the floor in front of my seat. The hatch cover could be locked and unlocked by four latches.

Other kayaks have nets or pouches along the sides and attached to the seat.

Regardless of the types of storage built into a kayak, there is much less storage than is found in boats. There are various ways to add storage to a kayak. One of the more popular approaches is to place a milk crate or other similar sized box behind the seat. Often vertical rod holders are attached. I will say more about crates and storage boxes in a later chapter.

The cockpit area of a kayak is nearly always crowded. It is difficult to keep tackle and tools in place, move yourself with paddle or pedals, and bring a fish into the cockpit area.

Stability, Seaworthiness, and Exposure to the Elements: Most fishing kayaks sit low to the water and offer good stability. Those that have elevated seats have a higher center of gravity. Under mild and moderate conditions, most kayaks are quite seaworthy. I have paddled and pedaled kayaks in up to 2' seas without concern about capsizing. That does not guarantee that users will never tip over. The key to staying upright is to keep your body weight as close to the center line of the kayak as possible. Those who lean out to the side to retrieve items from the rear storage area or to grab an incoming fish run the risk of being in a poorly balanced situation.

Some kayak anglers want to stand in their kayaks for casting. I do not have good balance and have no interest in standing in a kayak. But for those who do stand, paying attention to your body position and center of gravity are important factors.

Kayaks do not offer cabins, windscreens, or curtains to shelter the user from weather conditions. There is no substitute for common sense and good judgement when deciding whether to go out on the water or whether to continue on the water as weather conditions become worse.

Seating Comfort: A few kayaks have very comfortable seats, but many do not. It is quite important to be comfortable in the sitting position for at least several hours. If you get a sore butt or get wet on each outing, you are less likely to continue in the sport.

My first kayak (Ocean Kayak Drifter) did not come with a padded seat. It had a seating well molded into the plastic. When buying the kayak, I also bought a clip-in seat with a tall seat back. That particular kayak tended to accumulate water in the seating well. I added a throwable boat cushion under the seat. It helped keep me dry, but was not very comfortable.

My next kayak (Native Manta Ray 14) had a very nice padded and sloped seat that kept me comfortable for extended periods. The floor of the cockpit was graded so that most water entering the cockpit drained forward away from the seat and kept me dry.

My third kayak (Native Slayer Propel 13) had an upright "lawn chair-style" seat. It had an adjustable back. The raised seat allowed for tackle tray storage under the seats and a dry ride.

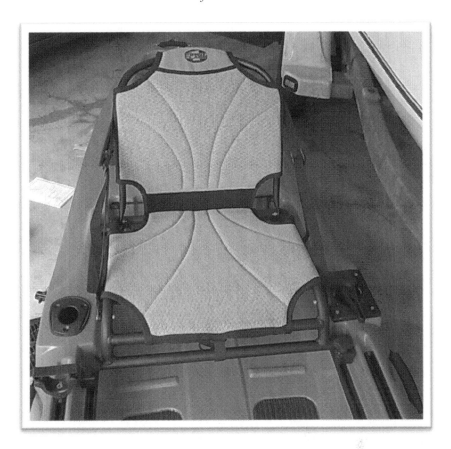

Seating comfort is important. Not all seats are created equal. Doing some homework and actually sitting in the kayak seats in the showroom can help determine what is right for you.

Limited Range: Before buying my first kayak, I fished in boats that allowed me to cover dozens of miles in a trip. At my age, covering 10-15 miles in a fishing kayak (not in a faster, narrower touring kayak) is the upper limit. Recognizing this limitation, I need to plan trips where the fishing grounds are relatively close to the launch point. I have had good success finding such spots. However, once committed to a launch point, you may be constrained about the different ways in which you can fish that day.

Limited Visibility to Other Boaters: Kayaks sit low in the water. Even kayaks with brightly colored hulls are not always visible to other boaters at a distance. Some kayakers install a flag pole and flag at the rear of their kayaks. This helps to improve visibility. Those who fish at night must show a white light. Some flag poles have lights on top for night use. The next photo shows a flag on Harry Steiner's kayak.

Photo Credit: Mark Bange

In my opinion, the first thing seen by a distant boat is not the kayak itself, but rather are the two paddle blades moving up and down. I strongly recommend getting paddles with bright colored blades (yellow, orange, white). If you use a black carbon fiber paddle like I do, add some colored and reflective tape to enhance visibility.

If you are in a pedal-powered kayak and have the paddle stowed, you can quickly pick up the paddle and wave it around to get the attention of an oncoming vessel.

Chapter 12 – Choosing a Kayak for Fishing

When I bought my first kayak in 2001, there were relatively few companies making fishing-friendly sit-on-top kayaks. Over the next 15 years, the kayak fishing sector of the fishing business exploded, bringing many new companies and kayak models to the marketplace. When I bought my first kayak, my main concern was finding one that was stable and could support the weight of my large body. Since then, the selection of kayaks suitable for fishing has grown to the point where it becomes confusing for first-time buyers. This chapter reviews some of the factors to consider when shopping for your first or your next kayak. A key point to remember is that there is no perfect boat for everyone. Each person has his/her own criteria that are weighted differently to decide which particular kayak is the best choice.

<u>Kayak Style</u>

Most kayak anglers fish from sit-on-top kayaks. Sit-on-top kayaks are designed for the user to sit on top of a hull in a seat. There is no part of the hull covering your legs.

Most sit-on-top kayaks have a series of drain holes in the floor called scuppers that allow water to exit the hull in case a wave or wake splashes inside the kayak. Sit-on-top kayaks offer a more open deck area for storing gear.

Some kayak anglers fish from sit-inside kayaks that have a large opening for the seat. The legs extend up under the top deck. Sit-inside kayaks are usually lighter than sit-on-top kayaks giving them greater speed through the water. They do not have scupper drains – carrying a pump or bailing device is a good idea in case a wave dumps water inside. Scott Taylor fishes from a sit inside kayak – he catches plenty of fish from that boat.

Photo Credit: Mark Bange

Canoes have served as good fishing platforms for decades. Stand up paddleboards (SUPs) have become quite popular for water recreation. Some SUP owner rig their boards with a cooler and rod holders and are able to fish from them. But a very large percentage of paddle craft anglers choose sit-on-top kayaks.

<u>Method of Propulsion</u>

Most kayaks are powered by double-bladed paddles. This is the traditional method of propulsion. Two leading companies offer foot pedal drives – Hobie and Native Watercraft. Pedal drives offer several advantages. First, leg muscles are usually stronger than arm muscles giving more propulsive force. Second, your hands are free to use fishing rods. Third, even if the pedal drive breaks or your legs get tired, you can still move under paddle power (assuming a paddle is carried).

Hobie's Mirage drive uses a front-to-back pedaling motion that drives two fins laterally underneath the hull. Mark Bange uses a Mirage drive on his Hobie.

Photo credit: Mark Bange

Native's Propel drive uses a bicycle pedaling motion that drives a two-bladed propeller under the hull, as shown in my Native Slayer Propel 13 kayak.

The Hobie drive moves the kayak forward, but the Native drive can go in forward and reverse. The models that offer pedal power are significantly more expensive than paddle-powered models.

A small subset of kayak anglers augment their standard propulsion system by adding an electric motor. This extends the range for a trip. Several companies make motors specifically designed for kayak use. Other kayak anglers modify regular electric trolling motors to work on their kayaks. Heavy batteries are needed to power the motors. This is a tradeoff – personally I have no desire to install an electric motor on my kayaks.

Paddle Selection: If you have a pedal-drive kayak, you should always carry a paddle with you in case of emergency. But it does not need to be an expensive paddle. If you use a paddle-powered kayak, you will use a paddle throughout your trip. Weight does make a difference. The paddle is moved back and forth hundreds of times each trip – a few ounces more of weight contributes to tiredness and soreness by the end of the day. Paddles range in cost from less than $50 to more than $500. The difference in cost relates to the materials (aluminum shafts with plastic blades are inexpensive but heavy; carbon fiber shaft and blades are much lighter and more costly).

Other features to consider when choosing a paddle are the shaft length and surface area of the blade. Shaft length should be determined by the height of the paddler (distance from shoulder to water), the width of the kayak (wider kayaks need longer shafts), and the primary style of stroke used (vertical stroke uses shorter shaft; horizontal stroke uses longer shaft).

The blade surface area is a matter of personal preference. Greater surface area provides more thrust per stroke, but requires more effort to pull the paddle. Typically paddles with larger blade area are used by paddlers preferring a vertical stroke pattern, whereas paddles with smaller blade area are used by those with a horizontal stroke pattern. I am very tall in the sitting position. I prefer a large blade area and a long shaft. I could not find a stock paddle that offered that combination in a lightweight carbon fiber material. My local kayak shop worked with me to special order a longer-than-usual shaft (240 cm) to go with a large blade on my new paddle – a custom Werner Ikelos model.

Seating Position and Comfort

In the previous chapter I discussed the importance of having a comfortable seat. The time to reach "butt fatigue" determines the length of time you can stay on the water, and often relates to how often you decide to fish from your kayak.

Some seat styles offer better lower back support. Anglers using pedal-drive kayaks should make sure they can remain comfortable with outstretched legs for extended periods while pedaling.

I usually add a gel-filled pad on top of the kayak seat to provide additional cushioning.

Transportation and Storage

Two very important considerations about choosing a kayak model are how will you transport it from your home to the water and how and where will you store it at your home. Fishing kayaks range in length from less than 10' to more than 15'. Most are 12' to 14'. Those kayaks range in weight from less than 50 pounds to more than 120 pounds. Most fall in the range of 60 to 80 pounds.

Hauling: Many kayak anglers employ roof racks for transporting their kayaks. Kayaks can be laid directly on the rack crossbars, or various types of cradle supports can be bolted to the crossbars. Once on the racks, the kayaks are held in place by ratcheting or cam-lock straps running from side-to-side. Some people add ropes from the bow and stern of their kayaks to minimize front-to-back movement.

Pickup truck owners often slide their kayaks into the bed. Most kayaks will hang out several feet past the tail gate. To provide additional support, bed extenders that fit into a hitch receiver can be used.

Photo Credit: Ben Morton

In February 2016, Mark Bange, John Rentch, and I spent the day fishing with Native Pro Staff member Todd Terrill near Palmetto, FL. Todd has an innovative way of hauling four paddle kayaks in the bed of his pickup truck. When needed, he can carry several other kayaks on the roof racks.

Photo Credit: Mark Bange

I carry my 10' and 11' kayaks inside the minivan. I experimented with various combinations of folding seats flat and removing seats to develop loading patterns that allow me to fully close the rear hatch.

Some kayakers who have heavy kayaks or who carry more than one kayak use trailers to transport their kayaks to the launch points. Some trailers are designed specifically for kayaks, while others are utility or boat trailers that were modified to carry kayaks. One downside to using a trailer is that some popular launch points in the Annapolis area do not allow trailer parking.

The welded aluminum trailer in the photo belongs to Neil Taylor. It was custom built for him by Kayracks to store his extra kayaks and to haul multiple kayaks when guiding large groups of clients.

Photo Credit: Neil Taylor

Storage: Those kayak anglers who have garages at their homes often store their kayaks inside the garage on the floor, on racks, or suspended from the ceiling by pulleys. I am fortunate to have a walkout basement. I store my kayaks on carpet strips laid on the basement floor.

If your home does not have inside storage space, it is necessary to store the kayak outdoors. Extended exposure to sunlight can degrade the plastic hull material. Covering the kayak with a roof, cover, or tarp is a good idea.

Carts and Trolleys: At some launch points, it is possible to back up to the edge of the water and slide the kayak directly into the water. But in most locations, it is necessary to move the kayak a few feet to hundreds of feet to reach the water. If you have a regular fishing partner, you can help each other carry the kayaks. But most kayak anglers use some type of cart or trolley to roll the kayak to the water.

One common style of cart uses two upright posts that slide into the scupper drain holes.

The other style cradles the hull against a frame. Both types include large-diameter wheels to roll the kayak across hard surfaces. If you plan to do a lot of beach launches, using large balloon tires makes rolling easier over sand.

How You Plan to Use It

It is useful to have an idea of where and how you plan to fish with your kayak. If you will only fish in ponds and lakes with calm water, you have a wider selection to choose from. If you want to head out into the main Chesapeake Bay on days with rough water and large waves, you will have fewer options that will allow you to go there and back safely.

If you plan to fish in free-flowing rivers with numerous rocks or want to fish next to bridge pilings, you may be better off with a used boat that already has some scratches in it.

Consider if you plan to make short trips (1-2 hours) or if you are more likely to spend many hours in the kayak and cover a lot of ground. If you plan to make long trips, a kayak that paddles easily or offers pedal power may be a good choice.

Longer kayaks tend to have greater weight capacity, track better, and are usually faster than shorter kayaks. But shorter kayaks are usually more maneuverable. Some models of kayaks come with rudders – for other models, rudders are an option to add later. Wider kayaks are generally more stable than narrower ones, although the shape of the hull plays a role in stability too. Because more of the hull is in contact with the water, wider kayaks tend to be slower than narrower ones.

If you want to stand up to cast, make sure the kayak model you choose has a flat floor area and good stability.

Other Decision Criteria

Some buyers look just at one or two brands of kayaks because those are the brands their fishing buddies already own. There is nothing wrong with that. Just make sure that you are choosing a kayak that works as well for you as it does for your buddy.

Some folks really want a new, shiny kayak -- that is important to them. Keep in mind that new kayaks, even when on sale, will be more costly than used kayaks of the same model. Often the used kayaks have accessories already installed. Try to determine your maximum budget capability then see what you can find in both new and used models. If you don't mind some scratches, you can get much more value for your money by buying a used, fully-rigged kayak. If you choose to buy new, be prepared to include the cost of a paddle, seat, and PFD to the cost of the kayak.

Consider the type and amount of storage and accessory mounts already on the kayak. Many newer kayak models have several lengths of gear track already installed. This allows much greater flexibility when installing or attaching accessories. Look for flush mount rod holders, cup holders, and other structures molded into the hull. The kayak shown below has three sets of gear tracks on each side plus two shorter ones that run laterally behind the black hatch cover. I mounted fishfinder/GPS units, rod holders, and paddle holders on these tracks. It also has one flush mount rod holder next to the seat, and a molded-in cup holder.

Making Your Decision

Each potential kayak buyer should identify the subset of criteria that are most important to them. Compare the models that best match those criteria, do some homework by reading, talking to others, and seeking information on kayak fishing chat boards like www.snaggedline.com – in my opinion the best online kayak fishing forum for the Chesapeake Bay region. Plan to visit a kayak dealer or the seller of a used kayak so you can look at the boats, sit in them, and check out how well you fit in the seat. If possible, arrange to take a test ride on the water before deciding.

Often cost is the deciding factor. When evaluating cost, consider the type of dealer from which you buy. Big box stores and online sales vendors often have attractive prices, but their salespersons generally are not as experienced in kayak usage and maintenance as those found at smaller kayak sales and rental shops. If you do need help later on with a warranty issue or need to get parts and accessories, there can be value to having a pre-existing relationship with a local dealer.

In calculating total cost, consider what extras are included in the purchase price. You definitely need a paddle, seat, and PFD. Some dealers may include these – others will not. Some dealers may offer a discount on accessories you buy along with the kayak or in the next few months. It pays to ask questions and explore options.

When I bought a new minivan in July 2015, I asked permission of the salesperson to try to load both of my smaller kayaks inside the van. In the parking lot of the dealership, I removed one of the van's seats and folded the other seats to try to load my first kayak. I then drove home, brought back my other small kayak, and tried loading it. The seating configuration and angle of seatback tilt were different on the new minivan compared to my old one. But with some trial and error, I found that I could indeed get the smaller kayaks fully inside. My behavior was a bit unconventional, but that helped me make my buying decision.

Chapter 13 – Rigging a Kayak for Fishing

It is a great day when you bring home your new or new-to-you kayak. Before using it for serious fishing, it is prudent to stop and evaluate what things you <u>must</u> have, and which other things you would like to have to make your fishing experience better or more productive. This chapter reviews the bare necessities and many other optional items.

Before buying and installing lots of accessories, it is wise to use the kayak for several trips to see how well you fit in the boat, what accessories are really needed, and where you would like to have the accessories installed for easy access from a sitting position. Before permanently installing any items that require drilling holes in the hull, think carefully about where you want those items to be. Measure several times to make sure you like the position then proceed.

<u>Basic Gear for Kayak Fishing and Safety</u>

Most kayak fishermen bring along lots of gear and accessories. Most of these items are not necessary to go kayak fishing – rather they make the experience more enjoyable, comfortable, and productive. In this section I cover those items that are absolutely necessary to bring on every trip. I subdivide the necessary items into those needed to paddle or pedal your kayak safely and legally and those that are needed for fishing.

What I Need to Operate a Kayak: At a minimum, you will need your kayak and a paddle. Paddles should be carried onboard even if your kayak is a pedal-drive or electric-motor-drive model. Some kayak anglers carry a spare paddle in case their main paddle breaks or is lost.

Many models of kayak come with a standard seat. If you buy a basic model, it may not have a seat or may have a seat that gets uncomfortable after a few minutes. Make sure you have a seat that allows you to sit and paddle comfortably.

You should always carry a personal flotation device or PFD. You can buy a wide range of PFDs from the basic orange style that slips over your head to fancy vests designed specifically for kayaking. Kayak fishing PFDs are designed with pockets or points of attachment for tools and safety equipment. The photo shows Terry Hill wearing a kayak fishing vest. He attached pliers and a hemostat to the vest. The pockets allow storage of other gear. My personal PFD is bright orange for the added visibility it offers.

Photo Credit - Mark Bange

Inflatable PFDs have grown in popularity too, but will not provide flotation unless they can inflate automatically or the user blows into a tube to inflate them. It is wise to check your state laws about PFDs. Some states require that inflatable PFDs be worn at all times if they are used as a primary PFD.

PFDs only work if you are wearing them – from a safety perspective, it makes sense to wear your PFD at all times. It doesn't matter if you are a good swimmer if you are unconscious from a medical emergency or an accident.

You are required to have a noise-making device onboard. Most kayak anglers attach a whistle to their PFDs. Other users bring separate horns with them.

If fishing at night, you are required to carry an approved 360° visual signal. Most kayak anglers use a high powered flashlight on a pole behind them or a headlight. I do not use my kayak in the dark, so I do not worry about that. Some users like to "pimp their ride" by adding strings of LED lighting to their kayaks.

In Maryland, boat registration is not required for vessels powered by paddle or pedal drives. However, those who operate electric-motor-powered kayaks must register their kayaks with the DNR.

While not a legal necessity, it is a good idea to carry water and a snack. If you stay out fishing for more than a few hours, you may want to carry multiple water bottles and snacks.

You should also carry one or more devices that allow you to communicate with others. I carry a cell phone at all times and often carry a handheld VHF radio in a pocket of my PFD. Various types of waterproof cases are available to protect cell phones. I have not needed the radio for safety reasons yet and hope I never need it for that purpose. It is very useful for keeping in touch with my kayak fishing buddies who are fishing in nearby areas out of direct talking distance. We can share fishing results from hundreds of yards away.

What I Need for Fishing: In order to go fishing, you need very little equipment. You must carry at least one rod and reel and have a minimal selection of tackle – lures or hooks and bait. You also need to have a valid fishing license for the waters where you plan to fish (you need to consider which state you are in, whether you are in tidal or non-tidal waters, and whether your license has reciprocity with another state in whose waters you are fishing).

Most people who take up kayak fishing are likely to want to do more than the most basic types of fishing. They will bring multiple rods, many tackle boxes or trays, and a variety of other fishing gear. These are discussed more in the following section.

| |

Other Types of Gear for Kayak Fishing and Safety

The previous section covered the most basic types of gear needed to get started in kayak fishing. This section discusses other items that are used by many kayak anglers.

Items for Safety and Comfort: In the Chesapeake Bay region, kayak anglers often share the water with other boaters. Kayaks are not as visible to other boaters as are larger vessels. There are advantages to making yourself more visible. I discussed this point previously. Unless you feel you need to blend in with the background for hunting or other reasons, brightly colored hulls and PFDs can be seen more easily than neutral colored ones.

It is a good idea to carry a basic first aid kit. Bandaids, antiseptic cream, adhesive tape, and superglue (for holding wounds together as well as for temporary repairs) can be very helpful in cases of minor cuts and scrapes.

A knife, scissors, and/or pliers are important both for fishing and for safety. At least one of those three should be available. I carry a pair of corrosion resistant pliers, a fish grip tool, a line cutter, a small pocket knife, and a Leatherman multi-tool.

In addition you may consider carrying a small tool kit and some critical spare parts, particularly if you are using a pedal-powered kayak. On one trip last summer, a bolt came loose on the seat of my kayak, making it difficult to sit upright and pedal. Fortunately I was able to grab my paddle and move to a sandy shoreline. I beached the kayak and used the Phillips head screwdriver on the Leatherman tool and my fishing pliers to re-tighten the bolt and nut. Without having both devices with me, I would have needed to end my trip prematurely. After that I made a tiny tool kit that I carry in my Plano waterproof tackle tray along with the Leatherman tool and a spare seat strap. The Allen wrenches, screw driver, spare shear pin and prop screw fit into the small plastic box on the left. These allow me to remove a propeller in case I get fishing line wrapped around the prop shaft, adjust my steering cable, and repair broken straps.

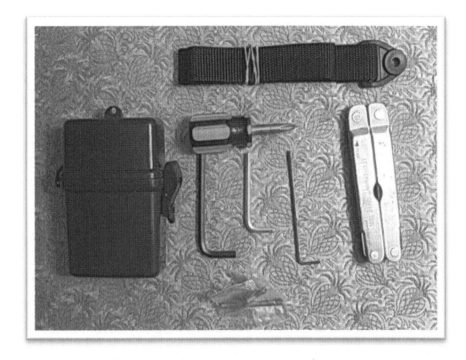

Other items that could come in handy are a spare set of clothes in a dry bag and a hand-operated pump to remove water that gets inside the hull. The latter is particularly important when using a sit-inside kayak.

If you plan to stay out on your kayak for more than a few hours at a time, consider purchasing a separate seat cushion that improves sitting comfort and extends the time to "butt fatigue". I use a Skwoosh gel-filled pad on my kayaks. As an aside, the same pads are helpful to improve seat comfort on airplane flights.

One other item is used by many kayak anglers to move their kayaks from their vehicles to the water's edge. This is a cart or trolley. Many styles and brands of these are available. Some have vertical posts that fit through scupper holes. Another style cradles and supports the kayak. These were discussed previously.

Fishing Related Items: As mentioned in the previous section, fishing can be very simple with a single rod and a few lures, or it can be a much more intensive activity. Most serious kayak anglers add accessories to their kayaks to make their fishing more effective. Here are some examples.

Most fishermen want to bring multiple rods with them. On a kayak with limited space, it is necessary to have a plan for how and where the rods not in use will be stored. Many users add rod holders to their kayaks. These can be flush mounted into the hull or can be bolted onto the surface of the hull. If you attach items to the hull, use stainless steel fasteners. Where possible, use bolts, washers, and nuts rather than screws. Other kayak anglers have designed elaborate rocket launchers out of PVC pipe that hold multiple rods for storage or trolling. Some rod holders are fixed in one position but others, such as the Scotty products I use, can be adjusted horizontally and vertically to allow the rods to assume many different angles depending on how they are deployed for trolling or other use. My personal preference is to store my rods in line with the hull and mostly horizontal when moving along and not trolling. I rotate the front rod holders so the rods point to the bow and the rear rod holders so the rods point to the stern. When I am ready to troll, I rotate the rods out to the sides at a 45 degree angle.

Most kayak anglers bring a large array of lures and other tackle with them. In the cramped confines of a kayak, it is imperative to develop a system for storing the tackle when it is not in use. Many kayak anglers add a milk crate or other box behind their seats to store tackle trays. Vertical tubes may be attached to the milk crates to provide additional rod storage.

John Rentch uses a milk crate on his kayak for rod and tackle storage.

Photo Credit: Mark Bange

Mark Bange started out using a milk crate but switched to a plastic BlackPak box specifically designed for kayak storage. In addition to holding tackle and other gear, that box accommodates mounting brackets for multiple rod holders.

Other kayak designs, particularly those with raised seats, allow storage of tackle trays beneath or behind the seat. Some kayak models have compartments with hatches built into the decks. Anglers can use these for storing small amounts of tackle.

If you store gear behind you such that you need to turn and reach around to access it, you should do your best to keep most of your body mass between the gunwales. Twisting and leaning out to the side to grab gear raises your potential for taking a spill, particularly when your kayak is heavily loaded with gear.

Another common accessory for fishing kayaks is an electronic fishfinder for observing bottom contours. Most modern units include GPS capability in the same unit. Users can switch back and forth between screens showing the fishfinder view, the GPS mapping view, or can use a split screen showing both at the same time. I use all three views depending on my needs at a specific point in the trip.

I use the fishfinder screen for finding fish in water deeper than 10', for seeing the bottom contour, and to know whether I am over level bottom, a slope, or near some type of structural feature like a mound or hole. The GPS screen tells me how fast I am moving, where I am in relation to land features and underwater features, and where I have already been. I try to use as much of this information as possible to follow my fishing plan and make adjustments when on the water.

These machines range from starter units with small black and white screens to larger color units with down scan and side scan capability. When fishfinders and GPS units are added to a kayak, it is necessary to provide a battery to power them. Placement of the screen unit, the transducer, and the battery on the kayak is subject to personal preference.

In 2015, I installed a new fishfinder/GPS unit in my Native Slayer Propel 10 kayak. I made a detailed YouTube video showing how I made the installation and why I chose to do it that way (https://www.youtube.com/watch?v=XdT4koUEnik). There are many ways to install electronics, but that video can serve as a starting point.

When landing fish and removing hooks, having a good pair of fishing pliers and some type of lip gripper device comes in handy. Lip grippers can be metal devices like a Boga grip or a plastic locking device like a Fish Grip. The wire device on the left is a jaw spreader tool that I use when pickerel fishing.

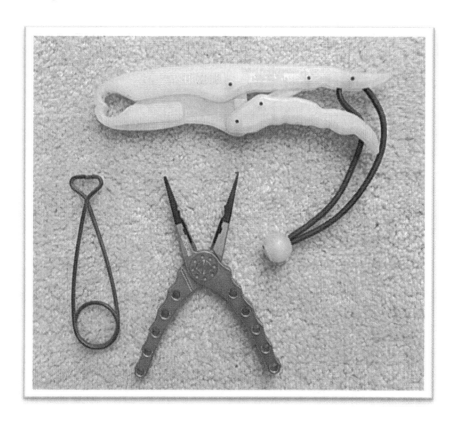

In some fishing situations, there are advantages to holding your kayak in one place. Many kayak anglers carry a small folding anchor and install an anchor trolley (a cord stretched between pulleys on the side of their kayaks). The anchor trolley allows adjustment of the angle at which the kayak sits in relation to the wind. The photo of Neil Taylor's kayak shows the dark-colored anchor trolley running along the side.

In the Chesapeake Bay region anchoring is not used as frequently as it is in some other regions – I use an anchor about once a year when fishing in my home waters. Nevertheless it does provide an additional degree of control of your kayak. In addition, kayak anglers can use stake-out poles or a mechanical anchoring accessory that lowers a pole into the bottom. Anchoring is a useful capability, but caution is needed when anchoring in flowing rivers or in areas of strong current. If current becomes too strong, the anchor and line can capsize a kayak.

Deploying drift socks or dragging lengths of chain can slow down the rate of drift. These are alternatives to anchoring.

Most kayak anglers enjoy having photos or videos of their fishing and catching. Photo capabilities range from cell phones to multiple video cameras mounted on poles allowing the angler to be the subject of the videos. Several vendors offer aftermarket mounting tools to hold cameras on your kayak or even on your head. I carry a water-resistant digital camera on a strap around my neck and tuck it into a shirt pocket. It is always readily available if I want take a shot of a fish I caught or some other object. I do not record video of my fishing trips, but many of the younger kayak anglers I see are enthusiastic about recording video clips of their exploits.

For those who plan to bring fish home to eat, having a cooler or fish bag filled with ice is desirable. Plus it keeps your drinks and lunch chilled. Others use a stringer to keep their catch alive until the end of a trip. I do not bring home any fish I catch on my kayak, so a cooler is not part of my kayak gear.

Nets help anglers land fish (particularly large fish or fish with lots of sharp teeth). However, in the close confines of a kayak, the mesh of the net can easily tangle with other gear and get in the way. If you use a net, consider how and where you will store it to minimize tangles. I do not carry a net with me in my kayaks, but Bruce Kellman has one with him in this photo.

Photo Credit: Mark Bange

Many kayak fishermen enjoy measuring the length of their catches, whether for personal enjoyment or for participation in a competition. The Hawg Trough (seen in many of the photos in this book) is one of the more popular measuring boards.

When live bait is used, anglers need a minnow bucket or a live well to keep the bait healthy and lively. Live wells require circulating water, which involves a pump and battery.

Final Thoughts on Gear

There is a trade-off between having lots of gear and accessories and how much time it takes to load and unload your kayak at the launch point. Excessive gear can get in the way and can weigh down your kayak. Each user must find his or her own comfort point on the spectrum from minimalism to overloading. I am very much on the minimalistic end of gear – I like to keep things simple and organized.

Part Five: Final Thoughts

Chapter 14 – Review of the Fishing Comfort Zone

This book covers a lot of material. The key point I want to pass on is that there are many ways in which to fish, lots of types of tackle and equipment, and many places to go fishing. None of us can fish in all ways and at all places. Some anglers love all forms of fishing, but most like some types better than others. To the extent that you can figure out which aspects of fishing you enjoy a lot and which ones you enjoy less, you can optimize your fishing experience by learning your personal fishing comfort zone.

The figure on the following page shows the concept of the fishing comfort zone.

Consider all the available methods for fishing. In my case, I don't choose to troll with heavy tackle, liveline, chum, or fly fish. Those fishing methods are excluded from my comfort zone.

Within the vast universe of fishing tackle, I do not fish with baitcasting or fly gear or with heavy tackle. I do not use crankbaits and other lures with treble hooks. I limit myself to light tackle spinning gear and just a few types of lures, mostly soft plastics. I use bait only in a few instances, not as a regular practice.

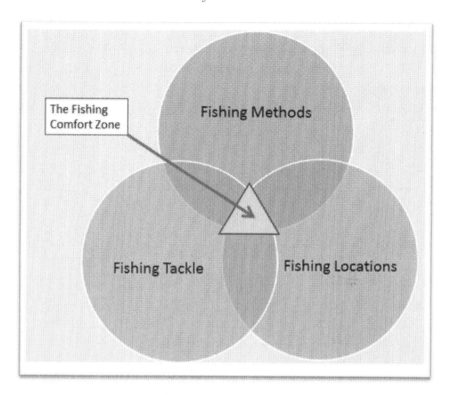

I do not like to travel far from home to fish on a regular basis. Most of my trips take place within 30 minutes driving time from my home. Most of my fishing is done in salt or brackish water settings. I do make several out-of-town fishing trips each year. When I go there, I almost always spend the night so I don't have long drives on the days on which I fish. I eliminated offshore fishing, driving to the mountains to fish for freshwater species, and long day trips from my comfort zone.

In each of these fishing sectors, I excluded large portions of the potential universe. The remaining portions of each sector overlap in the center of the diagram to form my fishing comfort zone.

My comfort zone evolved over many years of fishing. I have tried fishing in many ways with different tackle types and at different locations. I learned by trial and error and experience what I enjoyed and what I did not enjoy. I still make adjustments. From my interactions with the other

OGWLF members, each of whom has their own comfort zone that does not completely overlap with mine, I occasionally try something new. In May 2015, Mark Bange invited several of us to spend several nights at a state park in Delaware. We stayed in a cabin and a yurt and fished from our kayaks in the large lake. Since I planned to drive to Delaware anyway, I left home early on the first day and made a side trip to Lewes, DE where I caught several huge bluefish from my kayak. I probably would not have made the drive to Lewes just for the bluefish, but I included it as a part of another trip. Catching those big bluefish was one of the highlights of my fishing year in 2015.

Historically I fished primarily from my own power boats or on charter boats. Over the past decade, and especially since I retired from a full-time job in 2011, I make more and more trips from my kayaks and fewer from boats. I have strongly embraced kayak fishing as part of my fishing comfort zone. For that reason I devoted several chapters of the book to kayak fishing and how I choose to practice the sport.

Chapter 15 – Learning and Improving

I freely admit that I am not the world's greatest fisherman. Likewise I don't always catch the most fish or the largest fish. But I do catch quite a few fish and don't have many skunk trips anymore. My catching success has definitely improved from learning, making adjustments, practicing, and remembering what worked and what did not work. Following my retirement in 2011, I was able to change from fishing just on weekends to fishing year round 3 to 5 days a week, mostly on weekdays.

<u>Keys to Improving Your Fishing Skills</u>

Much of my improved fishing and catching success came from spending more time on the water. But simply going out day after day does not necessarily make someone a better fisherman. Here are some of the things I did that helped to make me more successful over time.

- *I tried to do homework before each trip.* I studied wind forecasts for speed and direction (www.windfinder.com), weather reports (www.weather.com), tide tables (www.tides4fishing.com), and online marine charts (http://webapp.navionics.com) to help plan my trip. When trying new locations, I looked on the charts for structural features that might hold fish. I considered how wind would affect water level in choosing which shorelines in a wide area would be more fishable under those conditions.

- *I paid close attention to the real-time data coming from my fishfinder/GPS machine.* In my center console, I watched for schools of bait and fish. In my kayak I watched speed, depth contours, and the tracks I made earlier in that day's trip and on previous trips. When fishing in a new area, I often entered several waypoints to mark spots where I caught the first few fish or caught several fish within an area.

- *I developed fishing patterns and routes that proved successful and tried to follow similar routes on successive fishing trips.* I trolled light tackle from my kayak at various depths until I discovered patterns and depths that worked most of the time on later trips. I learned specific locations or types of locations (e.g., creek mouths, points sticking into current, and oyster beds) that offered heightened potential for catching fish.

- *I extrapolated my own success or the successful reports made by other anglers to figure out how to fish new locations.* My early attempts at trolling from a kayak on the Susquehanna Flats led me to experiment in similar shallow-water habitats near the mouths of rivers closer to my home. This proved to be a great fishery on which I continue to fish frequently.

- *I learned from my less successful outings as well as from my highly successful ones.* Knowing that a technique or lure did not work on a trip allowed me to try to determine why it did not work and what I might do differently the next time out.

- *I experimented with different lures to improve my odds of catching fish.* I have a few dependable and successful lures that I use most of the time. Occasionally a friend gave me a new lure to try or I got some samples at a show. I tried to test the new lure in direct comparison with proven lures. For example, I have several types of small spinnerbaits that work well on perch. If someone gives me a different type of lure to test, I cast my old lure until I find where fish are biting. I cast the new lure to the same spot to see if the fish like that lure as well. I repeat this process several times to develop practical data on how well the new lure works. Or I may add a new lure to my light tackle trolling spread. I can easily determine how well it catches fish compared to the proven lures running alongside it.

- *I tried to develop relationships between where fish were biting at different tides, different water levels, different wind conditions, and different times of year.* This mental database is augmented by new information each year. For example, I usually stop trolling for stripers in the Severn by late September and shift over to casting for pickerel. On a trip in late September 2015, I had little success trolling in the main river. As I moved back to my launch point, I continued trolling. I was surprised to find large numbers of stripers above 20" in a tidal tributary where I had not previously looked for them. I continued LTT in the Severn River and other spots much later into the fall and found fish on many of those trips.

- *I learned tips from fishing buddies and professional guides with whom I fished.* For example, I began using a loop knot for most of my lures after seeing two different guides use that knot. My catching success improved after switching to the loop knot.

Why I Am Out There

I would not have worried about these details if I did not enjoy fishing. I rarely take fish home for the table – that is not why I am on the water so often. Instead I enjoy being in the beautiful habitats where I fish, observing the fish and other wildlife I see during the trips, and fishing with other like-minded fishing buddies. It has been rewarding to have catching success most of the time and to be able to share my knowledge with the OGWLF members as well as many others who I meet through online fishing forums.

Takeaway Points

It would be presumptuous of me to think that I have all the answers about how to be a successful fisherman. Many of the ideas and techniques I describe in this book are well known and commonly used by other anglers. I referenced several excellent books by local fishing writers – those guys along with most professional guides and charter captains are very skilled at fishing. Their approach to fishing has some overlap with my approaches, but each one of them has areas where they do things differently and maybe better. This is completely acceptable – they found their own fishing comfort zones and I found mine.

The photo shows a beautiful rainbow over one of my favorite local tidal creeks. That morning I trolled paddletails from my kayak in the light rain and caught a bunch of fat stripers in this scenic cove. That morning was definitely in my fishing comfort zone.

You do not need to own a large number of rods and reels, shelves full of tackle, or large and powerful fishing boats to be a successful and happy fisherman. Simplicity and knowing what I need to get the job done serves me well.

I encourage readers to learn from my book and from books by others. Attending seminars, reading online fishing chat boards, and fishing with skilled guides will help to improve your fishing skill set and allow you to refine your own fishing comfort zone.

Finally fish as often as your schedule and budget allows. The best way to get better at fishing is to keep practicing. Try to incorporate new techniques and tackle where they make sense. While you do that, try to understand why the new approach offers advantages to your old approach. And above all, be safe and have fun while you are fishing.

Photo Credit: Neil Taylor

About the Author

John Veil lives in Annapolis, Maryland with his wife Carol. He is an avid fisherman, kayaker, and boater. He spends several days a week fishing on the waters of the Chesapeake Bay, most often in the Severn River and its tidal creeks and ponds. Over the past five years he has spent an increasing proportion of his fishing time in kayaks. He serves on the Pro Staff team for Native Watercraft kayaks. Much of this book is focused on fishing from kayaks and other small boats.

Photo Credit: Neil Taylor

In addition to his passion for water recreation, his entire professional career has been spent on water-related issues. He previously worked in academia, as a state regulator, as a researcher, and currently is the president of a water and energy consulting practice - Veil Environmental, LLC.

Throughout his career, he has published numerous technical reports, papers, and book chapters, as well as making hundreds of technical presentations on water and energy subjects. He is a frequent contributor to Chesapeake Bay internet fishing forums. However, this book is his first formal effort at laying out his own fishing philosophy and practices.